Searchlights

The all-age resource for

Common Worship

Year B

David Adam

kevin mayhew

First published in 2005 by

KEVIN MAYHEW LTD
Buxhall, Stowmarket, Suffolk, IP14 3BW
E-mail: info@kevinmayhewltd.com
Web: www.kevinmayhew.com

9 8 7 6 5 4 3 2 1 0

ISBN 1 84417 428 X
Catalogue No 1500817

Artwork by Andy Robb
Cover design by Angela Selfe
Edited and typeset by Katherine Laidler

Printed in Great Britain

Contents

Introduction

Once pre-school children had little opportunity for communal learning. Now there are playschools, nurseries and pre-school groups. There are also many television programmes directed towards these young ones. It is important, therefore, that the church is a place where this learning is built upon and extended. Above all, these young children need to see the church as a place where they are welcome and they look forward to coming to. Atmosphere is of vital importance: the children need to know they are loved and accepted, that they are listened to and respected. The way we deal with these youngsters will affect their future attitude towards the church and at the same time show the importance of the church's mission and outreach to the young. The church may be the only place where there is a concern for their spiritual as well as their physical and educational growth. It is of the utmost importance that we give proper attention and resources to this privilege that is given to us.

Teachers need to be properly prepared and trained to do their work. They need to be given the necessary equipment to work properly. A draughty corner of a large room will not do. Chairs and tables that are right for the age group are necessary. The vicar and the PCC need to review regularly what is being done and encourage the teachers by their support and financial outlay. Teachers should be encouraged to go on courses and meet up with other teachers. They should also be given the opportunity to look at new teaching methods and materials. All this will show that we take the teaching of our pre-school children seriously.

The teaching itself needs to be fun. Much of it at this stage needs to be play-based with lots of activity. Remember, though, that children do love stories. Everything needs to be prepared carefully with the class or classes in mind. It may be necessary to split this age group into at least two groups. It is good always to have at least one of the parents to help with the supervision each week. Often a new child could have its parent stay for a session or two as a helper. It is a big step for the child to leave the protection of a parent and be handed over to someone whom they have never met. This is also a learning opportunity for the parent. All parents should be encouraged to come occasionally to help in the work of the group and to pray with their child at home.

Teachers should always read the passages of Scripture even if they will not be reading them to the children. Each week the ideas and the material are based on Common Worship Readings for the Sunday or for the current Church season. Well in advance the teachers need to know what visual aids are going to be used and what other resources are required. Vary the material used, such as finger paints, pastels, crayons, different paper colours and textures. Get the children to make simple musical instruments to play and banners to carry. In photocopying the material from this book sometimes it is good to make it A3 size rather than always A4. All the material is copyright-free for non-commercial use in the church, club or home.

The whole session needs to be prepared carefully. Imagine yourself in the story, maybe from the point of view of one person within it. Use each of your senses. What were the things that could be seen and heard? What did things feel or taste like? What did it smell like? This all helps the story to come alive. You could act out what was happening to an individual, or get the children to act out a story after it is told. Teach the songs carefully and make sure the children understand the words. It is good to use the song more than once. Sometimes the children should be able to sing their newly learnt song in church.

Pray for each of the children by name and their families in your own prayers. Talk to God about them. Come to God with the children in your heart. Come to the children with God in your heart. This may not instantly be seen but it will make a great difference.

David Adam

ADVENT
First Sunday of Advent

Aim
To prepare for the coming of Jesus.

Readings
Isaiah 64:1-9
Psalm 80:1-7,17-19
1 Corinthians 1:3-9
Mark 13:24-37

Teaching
This is Advent Sunday and it tells us someone is coming soon. Who is coming? When do we remember that Jesus is coming? Do you know how many Sundays there are in Advent? (Show the Advent Candles or hold up four fingers.) What happens after four Sundays?

When Jesus came, the night was dark. There were stars shining in the sky. If you looked out on the hills you could see shepherds guarding their sheep in case there were wolves or robbers. One young shepherd had to keep the light burning to scare away the darkness and the dangers. He liked to keep a great big fire burning. What do you think he put on the fire?

He put on a big piece of wood, a log – and he threw it on to the fire. He did not get too close because fire burns. Now he watched the sparks fly upwards like bright lights in the dark. They flew higher and higher right up into the sky. Joel – that is his name – watched the sparks rise into the night. He thought that they would go up higher and then go out, but he saw that they were getting brighter. The sky was being filled with light. It wasn't sparks he was watching; it was God's angels of light coming down from heaven. He began to hear them singing. The shepherds were nearly all asleep, they would miss the angels and their song – so Joel woke them up. Wake up! Wake up! The shepherds jumped up for they thought a wolf was coming. But they got a big surprise. Joel pointed upwards and they heard and saw angels in the sky. The angels were singing a beautiful song: 'Glory be to God in the highest and peace on earth.' Then the angels told them Jesus is coming and he is coming to Bethlehem. The shepherds were very excited and all of them wanted to go to Bethlehem and see Jesus.

Activities
We are going to make some shepherds to take into church, and later they will go and see Jesus. (Next week the children will make an angel; the third week, Mary and Joseph; and the fourth week, the baby Jesus and a star.) The figures can be coloured in and stuck to a piece of kitchen roll tube to make them stand. Each child should end up with a nativity group.

We will also colour in one candle to remind us that Jesus is coming and he comes to us.

Prayer
O God, you are always with us, even in the dark.
You come to us because you love us.
As you told the shepherds about Jesus,
help us to learn about his coming and his love for us.
Amen.

Song
Jesus bids us shine

Notes

1

Second Sunday of Advent

Aim
To prepare for the coming of Jesus.

Readings
Isaiah 40:1-11
Psalm 85:1-2, 8-13.
2 Peter 3:8-15a
Mark 1:1-8

Teaching
Have you ever been sent with a message or been asked to go somewhere and get something? It is important that messengers carry the right message and don't get it wrong. If you were sent to the kitchen for a biscuit and brought back some soap, it would be wrong.

God has often sent messages to people and he makes sure they get the right message. God calls his messengers 'angels'.

Once, long ago, God sent a messenger – one of his angels – to a little town called Nazareth, to the house of a young woman called Mary. The angel knew exactly which house to go to. Mary had been outside in the garden working, looking after plants. Now she was having a quiet time in the house, waiting until her mother came home. Suddenly she saw God's messenger in the room. The door was open and she did not hear the messenger knock or come in, but suddenly he was there. Mary was frightened and hid her eyes. But the angel said to her, 'Do not be afraid, Mary. I come from God and God is very pleased with you. God knows that you love him and try to do what he wants. He now wants you to do something special; he wants you to have a baby that you will call Jesus.'

Mary was not really sure what the angel meant and asked him. Meanwhile, God and the messenger waited for her answer. (If possible, show a picture of Mary with the angel.) The angel told Mary that God would make it happen and that she would be the mother of Jesus.

Mary said, 'I will do what God wants.' The angel was very happy and went back to God to say he had delivered the message. And all the angels rejoiced.

Activity
We are going to pass on a message from one to another. I will whisper it and pass it on. 'God loves you.' See if we get it right.

We will colour in an angel for our Christmas crib – let it be gold and silver, if possible. Do you remember whom the angel came to last week?

How many candles are there to colour in?

Prayer
God, we thank you
that you sent the angel messenger to Mary
and that she let Jesus be born into the world.
We will try to do what you want us to do
because we know that you love us.
Amen.

Song
Jesus bids us shine

Notes

1
2

Third Sunday of Advent

Aim

To continue with the Christmas story.

Readings

Isaiah 61:1-4, 8-11
Psalm 126 or the Magnificat
1 Thessalonians 5:16-24
John 1:6-8, 19-28

Teaching

Who can remember what we call God's messengers? The messengers were sent to the shepherds and to Mary. (If there is no reply, get them to look at the angels they have made.)

Mary told Joseph how the angel came to her and said that she would have a baby. Joseph wished the angel would come and speak to him. He looked for it all day but it did not come. Then at night, when it was dark and he was asleep, the angel came and spoke to him in a dream. The angel had a message for Joseph: 'Joseph, son of David, I want you to look after Mary and the baby she is going to have. You must call the baby Jesus because he will save his people.' When Joseph woke up he thought about his strange dream. He would look after Mary and call the baby Jesus.

Now Joseph had to get ready to go on a long journey and take Mary with him. They were going to go from Nazareth, where they lived, right down to Bethlehem to have their names written in a book. It was about 76 miles. If we had to go that far we would go by car or by train. Joseph would walk and Mary would walk with him or ride on their donkey. They would have to walk every day for a whole week. They would be very tired. Mary would be especially tired because her baby was soon to be born.

Near the end of the week they went past Jerusalem. There were lots of other people walking and riding camels, horses or donkeys. They had six miles to go and they were very slow because Mary could not go any faster. Joseph looked after her and helped her. At last they could see Bethlehem and they could see the fires in the hillsides where the shepherds were looking after their sheep.

It was now quite dark. Joseph looked up at the stars and said thank you to God that Mary had got safely to Bethlehem; it would be good if her baby was born there.

Activity

We are going to colour in Joseph and Mary and then we will colour in three candles for three Sundays in Advent. Do you know how many more Sundays there are in Advent?

Prayer

God, we thank you for the message of the angels
and for Mary and Joseph.
As we look forward to Christmas
help us to know that Jesus comes to us.
Amen.

Song

Jesus' love is very wonderful

Notes

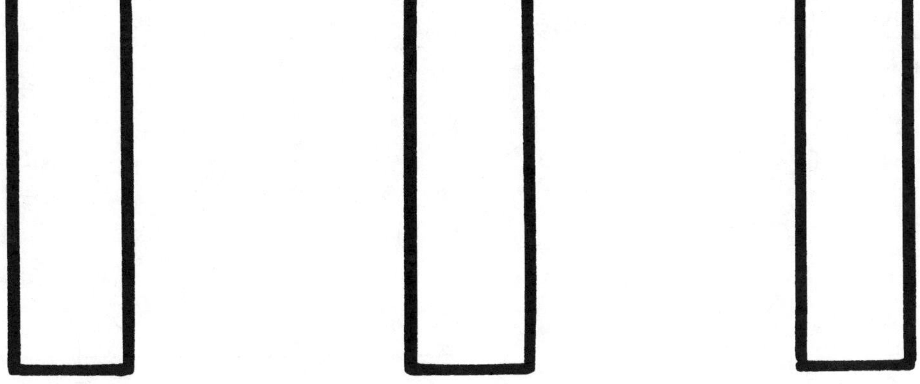
1
2
3

Fourth Sunday of Advent

Aim
To enter into the joy of the coming of Jesus.

Readings
2 Samuel 7:1-11, 16
Magnificat or Psalm 89:1-4, 19-26
Romans 16:25-27
Luke 1:26-38

Teaching
Can you remember last week when Joseph and Mary set off to walk to Bethlehem? Well, they have walked all week except Saturday, the Sabbath, when they worshipped in the synagogue (church). Every day, Monday to Friday, they walked miles. When Mary was tired she sat on the donkey but she walked a good bit of the time. Now she was very tired – and the donkey was tired. They were walking more slowly than most other people, and it would be getting dark when they arrived in Bethlehem. The stars were coming out in the sky and they could see the fires the shepherds had lit in the hills to frighten away wild beasts. Joseph wished Mary would go a little faster but knew she could not for she was soon to have her baby. When they got to Bethlehem all the inns were full of people. At the last place they tried, Mary could hear the noise and the singing, the place was crowded; she prayed that she could have somewhere quiet.

Joseph brought the innkeeper to see Mary. He explained that there was no room, but he had a quiet cave behind the inn. If Mary did not mind sharing it with the cow and the hens, she could make herself comfortable there. How pleased Mary was: this was better than a noisy inn. Now she could settle down.

As she rested she listened to the cow munching hay and the hens quietly clucking.

She knew the time had come: the baby Jesus was to be born in the stable. She was so happy. There in the quiet, with Joseph looking after her, the baby Jesus came, and Mary and Joseph gave him their love. Mary hugged the baby and said, 'Hello, Jesus.'

Activity
We know that Jesus was born on Christmas Day. Let us colour in the picture of Jesus lying in the cradle of hay. Then we will put all our nativity figures together so that we can take them into church (or take them home). Some of the figures could be used on Christmas Day. If there is time, let the children talk about the crib figures.

Prayer
God, we thank you
for the coming of Jesus into the world
and for loving us.
Amen.

Song
Away in a manger

Notes

1
3
2
4

First Sunday of Christmas

Aim

To share in the wonder of Christmas.

Readings

Isaiah 61:10–62:3
Psalm 148
Galatians 4:4-7
Luke 2:15-21

Teaching

Go over the Christmas story of the angels appearing to shepherds. Tell of the angels singing, 'Glory to God in the highest', and of the shepherds deciding to go and see the baby. Then tell of the visit to Mary, Joseph and the baby Jesus.

Then let the children act out the story. Have a few tea towels for head-dresses for the shepherds. Maybe dress the angels in white (choir surplices are ideal). Joseph and Mary could be in their ordinary clothes, and Mary could have a doll for Jesus.

Ask the children, 'Who would like to be an angel?'

Who would like to be a shepherd? Who would like to be Mary and Joseph?

Set the scene by telling them the shepherds were sitting and sleeping around the fire, and some were watching the sheep. Give the shepherds time to do this. 'Then an angel appeared and said . . .' Let the children use their own words. If they get stuck for words encourage them: 'A new baby has been born in Bethlehem. He is called Jesus. Go and see him.' Let the shepherds travel across the room to Mary and Joseph. As they travel, all could sing 'Here we go to Bethlehem'.

Allow the shepherds to comment on the baby, and encourage Joseph and Mary to welcome them. If there are too many children for all to take part, the play could be repeated with other children whilst the first actors watch.

Activity

Draw an angel using children's hands to draw around for the wings. Colour the angel in gold and use glitter to make it shine. If the angels are not to be taken home, they could be mounted on black paper to show them off. A few stars could be added to the paper.

Prayer

God, we thank you for the song of the angels
and for the shepherds seeing Jesus.
We come this day to give Jesus our love.
Amen.

Song

Here we go up to Bethlehem

Notes

The Angel of God

Second Sunday of Christmas

Aim

To let the children know that they are loved by God.

Readings

Jeremiah 31:7-14 and Psalm 147:12-20
or Ecclesiasticus 24:1-12 and Wisdom 10:15-21
Ephesians 1:3-14
John 1: (1-9) 10-18

Teaching

This is the story of a little boy who had lots of toys but he was very sad. He had enough food, nice clothes and lived in a big house but he was not happy. He thought that his mummy and daddy did not love him and he felt very lonely – all by himself. One night Mummy heard him crying because he was frightened of the dark. She came into the room put a light on and hugged him and kissed him. She told him how much she loved him and she stayed with him until he was asleep.

The next night his daddy came upstairs with him and told him a story. He also gave him a big hug and told him that he loved him. Then he told him how Mummy and Daddy would always love him and look after him. The little boy smiled because he was very happy. Everyone noticed the change. He was not afraid of the dark because he knew he was loved and that Mummy or Daddy would come if he needed someone.

God saw that lots of people were afraid of the dark and were sad and lonely, so he sent Jesus into the world to show that he loved them all. Jesus showed that God loves children and cares for people who are ill. God wants us to be happy.

Where was Jesus born? (Get the children to reply.) Who looked after him? (Mary and Joseph.) He loved them and they loved him. When he grew up, he would tell everyone that God loves them.

Let us sing 'Jesus' love is very wonderful'. We will stretch as tall as we can when we sing, 'So high you can't get over it'. Then we'll go down as low as we can when we sing, 'So low you can't get under it'. Then we will stretch our arms out wide when we sing, 'So wide you can't get round it'. Then we will hug ourselves when we sing, 'Oh wonderful love'.

Activity

We will colour in the words 'Jesus loves me' and the picture.

Prayer

God our Father, we thank you for your love.
Jesus loves us and we are happy.
We would like to give our love to you.
Amen.

Song

Jesus' love is very wonderful

Notes

Jesus loves me

EPIPHANY
The Epiphany

Aim
To encourage the children to offer themselves to God.

Readings
Isaiah 60:1-6
Psalm 72:(1-9) 10-15
Ephesians 3:1-12
Matthew 2:1-12

Teaching
Show a star. Do the children ever see stars? Do they know the names of any stars?

The wise men liked looking at the stars. One night they saw a very bright star – it looked bigger than all the others. They knew it was shining because someone important had been born into the world – a special baby – and they must go and see him. The wise men set off at night. (Why?) They travelled across the desert and for many miles until they came to Jerusalem. Here they were a little lost, so they asked someone the way. They asked the king but he was a wicked king and he did not know. The church people knew and said they would have to go to Bethlehem. It was only seven miles away, so they were lucky. (Compare distances to places near home.)

At last they came to where Jesus was. They each brought him a gift. Do you know what they were?

Activity
Have some gifts wrapped for the children to unwrap. Explain these are not gifts to keep but for them to look at. You could have many wrappings on the gifts and the children can pass around one gift at a time and unwrap a layer when the music stops. Each gift could be contained in a box. The gold could be a brooch or a ring. The frankincense could be some incense grains or an incense stick, which could be lit for them to smell. You may be able to get some myrrh from the chemists; if not, use a small medicine bottle filled with bits of silver paper. When all the gifts are unwrapped talk about them and why they were given to Jesus.

Colour the picture of the wise men bringing their gifts. Cut them out and stick each to a piece of kitchen roll tube so they stand up. The star could be stuck on to a longer piece of tube (black, if possible).

Prayer
Father, we thank you that the wise men found Jesus
and that the wicked king did not.
We would like to give Jesus our love this day.
Amen.

Song
Guide us, guide us little star,
we have travelled very far.
We have seen your lovely light
as we journey through the night.
Now we come to Christ our King
and our love to him we bring.

Let the leader sing a line (to the tune of 'Twinkle, twinkle, little star') and then the children echo it.

Notes

First Sunday of Epiphany
The Baptism of Christ

Aim

To let the children enter into the wonder of the baptism of Jesus.

Readings

Genesis 1:1-5
Psalm 29
Acts 19:1-7
Mark 1:4-11

Teaching

What do we use water for? Drinking and watering the garden, and many other things. Water gives life and refreshes us.

Did you know that water can destroy life? Floods and drowning – maybe someone knows the story of Noah.

Water washes, makes things clean. We should always wash our hands before meals.

Jesus had lived at his home in Nazareth until he was ready for the special work only he could do. At the beginning of his work he went to the river Jordan to be baptised in the water by John. This was a very special time for Jesus. John, in his rough clothes, led him into the river and dipped Jesus right under the water. This was to be a new start for Jesus, a new sort of life. As he was coming out of the water there seemed to be a hole in the sky and out of it came the Spirit of God, like a dove descending. He knew then that his special work was to begin. Then there came a voice from heaven – it was God the Father and he was speaking to Jesus. He said, 'You are my Son, the Beloved; with you I am well pleased.' What was God the Father saying to Jesus?

At the baptism of Jesus, the Father was heard to speak and the Spirit was seen coming upon him. What do we call the Father, Son and Holy Spirit?

Activity

In and out the Jordan

Make a circle with one person in the middle to give the commands – this may need to be the teacher for the first time. Children have to react to the words of the one in the middle. Tell them the Jordan is a river.

In the Jordan (everyone jumps in)
On the bank (everyone jumps out backwards)
On the Jordan (no one moves)
In the bank (no one moves)

Vary the order of these words. Anyone who makes a wrong move or wobbles is out. The last person left is the winner.

Prayer

Father, we thank you that you made us
and that you love us.
Jesus, we thank you that you came to earth for us
and that you love us.
Spirit, we thank you that you are ever with us
and that you love us.

Song

Father, we adore you

Notes

For parents and children to pray together
'Father, you love us,
Jesus, you love us,
Spirit, you love us.
We give our love to you.'
Stick some cling film or blue cellophane on to the water.

Second Sunday of Epiphany

Aim

To show that God cares for even the smallest of his children.

Readings

1 Samuel 3:1-10 (11-20)
Psalm 139:1-6, 13-18
Revelation 5:1-10
John 1:43-51

Teaching

Who has helped Mummy or Daddy at home? (Let the children talk about how they are helpful.)

Have you ever helped to clean the church? Some people do it every week. Wouldn't it be good if you could sweep the floors and hoover the carpets? If you were careful, you might be allowed to polish the pews or the brass. What we can all do in church is be very quiet and say our prayers. God likes to hear every one of us . . .

There was once a boy who lived in a church. He helped an old man called Eli to look after things. The boy's name was Samuel. (Show the children pictures of Samuel and Eli.)

'I like helping you,' Samuel said to Eli. 'Do you think God is happy with what I am doing?' Eli smiled because Samuel worked carefully. 'God is happy with the way you sweep the floor and keep the place tidy. God is happy that you help me and that you say your prayers. God loves you.'

Samuel was very glad that God loved him and it made him enjoy helping. What do you think Samuel did when it got dark? Yes, like you, he would go to bed. Here is a little mat that he used for a bed. It is not as nice as your bed but he found it very cosy.

One night Samuel went and lay down on his mat. (Let a child lie on Samuel's mat.) Eli went to bed in a different place at the other end of the church. Let us put Eli in his bed. Soon both were fast asleep.

Suddenly in the dark Samuel heard a voice calling his name. Let us say his name two times. 'Samuel, Samuel.' Who do you think was calling? Samuel thought it could only be Eli so he ran to the old man and woke him up and asked him what he wanted. 'You called me and here I am.' Eli said, '*I* did not call you. Go back to bed.'

Samuel went back to bed and was nearly asleep when the voice called again. Let us say it together: 'Samuel, Samuel.'

He ran to Eli woke him up and said, 'You *did* call me.' But Eli said, 'I *did* not. Go back to bed.'

Samuel went back to bed but before long do you know what happened? Yes. The voice called again – let us say the words: 'Samuel, Samuel.' Samuel again woke Eli. This time the wise old man knew that something special was happening. Who do you think was speaking to Samuel? Eli told Samuel to lie down again and if God called to say, 'Speak, Lord, for your servant is listening.'

Samuel lay down and was very quiet. He hoped God would call him again. He had never thought that God would bother with a little lad like him. But God cares for all his children – he cares for you. Samuel waited for a while (pause). Then God called again (let us say it together): 'Samuel, Samuel.' This time Samuel sat up and said, 'Yes, God, I am listening to you.' God told him some very special things that no one knew.

In the morning Samuel said to Eli, 'Isn't it wonderful? God has spoken to me even though I am still small. I know God loves me and I love him.'

Activity

Act out the following:

This is the way we sweep the floor,
sweep the floor, sweep the floor,
this is the way we sweep the floor
early in the morning.

Repeat with the following sentences:

This is the way we polish the pews . . .
This is the way we say our prayers . . .
This is the way we listen to God . . .

Prayer

Dear God, we thank you that you love all children,
that you hear our prayers and speak to us.
Amen.

Song

Two little eyes to look for God

Notes

Second Sunday of Epiphany (B)

Third Sunday of Epiphany

Aim

To show that the presence of Jesus brings joy.

Readings

Genesis 14:17-20
Psalm 128
Revelation 19:6-10
John 2:1-11

Teaching

Show a picture of a wedding. Who has been to a wedding? Maybe someone has been a bridesmaid or a pageboy? Weddings often begin in church when the bride and groom ask God to bless them and keep them happy together. After the church service there is a wedding party. There will be lots of nice things to eat and drink and everyone is happy. Who has been to a party?

Jesus went to a wedding at Cana. Jesus' mother was there (can you remember her name?) and so were some of the disciples. When they went to the house there were six great big pots of water near the door. (Count your six big water pots.) The water was used for washing hands and feet and lots of people had used it.

It was a lovely party. The bride and groom had crowns on their heads and were just like a king and queen. They were very happy (show bride and groom happy faces) and enjoying themselves. Jesus and the disciples were enjoying themselves too.

At the party, Mary told Jesus that they had run out of wine. There were no shops where they could buy more wine so the party would have to stop. This would make the bride and groom very sad (show bride and groom sad faces).

When Jesus heard this he asked that the water pots be filled up to the top with water. The servants obeyed Jesus and did what he asked. 'Now,' he said, 'give some to the man who is helping to organise the wedding.' Again, they obeyed Jesus. 'This is wonderful wine: the very best wine. It is better wine than we had at the beginning,' said the man. He did not know that Jesus had turned water into wine. The helpers who had obeyed Jesus knew and they smiled. The bride and groom also smiled (show the faces) because the party could keep going. Jesus had made everyone happy.

Let us smile because Jesus loves us and wants us to be happy.

Activity

Make happy and sad faces using paper plates. Colour in six large water pots, blue on one side and red on the other.

Let us pretend we are at the wedding and we are helping to wash people's hands and feet. Now let us obey Jesus.

'Fill the water pots with water.' (Show blue side or at this point colour them blue.)

'Take them to the man who is organising the wedding.' (Let another child be the man.)

When he tasted the water it had become wine. (Colour other side of pots.)

He said, 'This is lovely, give some to everyone.' (Pretend to pour out wine for all.)

To practise listening and obedience they could play 'Simon says'.

Prayer

Jesus, we thank you
for all the lovely things you do for us
and that you look after us.
Help us to look after others.
Amen.

Song

Jesus' love is very wonderful

Notes

Faces made from paper plates. Happy on one side. Sad on the other.
Draw six water pots. Colour blue on one side, red on the other.

Fourth Sunday of Epiphany

Aim

To show the love of Jesus as revealed in healing.

Readings

Deuteronomy 18:15-20
Psalm 111
Revelation 12:1-5a
Mark 1:21-28

Teaching

Jesus went to the synagogue (explain) on the Sabbath to teach people about the love of God. There were a lot of people there and some of them would be fishermen because Capernaum was beside the sea. All of them were dressed up in their best clothes for going to church. Jesus stood up to teach them and they all listened very carefully. They thought that he was a wonderful teacher and they would have been happy to listen to him all morning – all except for one man. He was a strange man and a bit of a wild man. No one was ever sure about what he would say or do. He suddenly shouted out in church, 'What have you to do with us, Jesus of Nazareth? Have you come to destroy us? I know who you are, the Holy One of God.'

Everybody was horrified at the noise the man made and wanted him to be quiet. Some wanted to get him to leave the church because he was being a nuisance. I wonder how many listened to his words. (Repeat the words.) He asked two questions and both were very wise. He asked, 'What have you come here for?' Well, Jesus had come to teach and to tell them about the love of God. Jesus had come because God loves everyone and he wanted these people to know it.

The other question was a bit strange: 'Have you come to destroy us?' Well, Jesus did not come to destroy anyone; rather, he came to set them free and help them lead a full life. Yet the man was right for Jesus came to fight against evil and sickness and anything that hurt people. This man was ill and needed healing. Jesus would seek to make him better.

There was something in this man that recognised Jesus as the Holy One of God. He knew who Jesus was and wanted to shout about it. A lot of people in church did not know who Jesus was. Jesus asked him to be quiet. And then he did something wonderful: he commanded the evil to come out of the man. Jesus' words were very powerful and the evil left the man and the man was made well.

Everyone in church was amazed. Jesus not only spoke about God but he acted like God. At once all over the area people were talking about Jesus. What do you think they were saying?

Activity

Let everyone run around until the music stops. Then they must be absolutely still. The next time the music starts only those touched by the leader can move. Leave only a few to be still each time. When the music stops all are still. Repeat this process. Only those touched by the leader are to move. Let them see that the leader brings freedom of movement.

Prayer

Jesus, we thank you for the stories you told
and all that you taught us.
We thank you that you healed people
and wanted them to enjoy living.
Amen.

Song

Jesus' hands were kind hands

Notes

God loves the world he made.

Draw something God loves

God wants us to be happy and healthy.

Draw a happy face

God loves us.

Can you write your name in the heart?

For parents and children to pray together

'God, thank you for loving us and wanting us all to be happy.'

The Presentation of Christ

To be used on the Sunday nearest to 2 February, if not on the day. There is no separate teaching for the children and young people as the service has action for all. If the groups need to go out they can use the illustration section and colour candle templates.

Notes

For parents and children to pray together

'Jesus, let your light shine upon us and our homes.'

ORDINARY TIME
Proper 1

Sunday between 3 and 9 February inclusive
(if earlier than the Second Sunday before Lent)

Aim
To show how Jesus loves and heals.

Readings
Isaiah 40:21-31
Psalm 147:1-12, 20c
1 Corinthians 9:16-23
Mark 1:29-39

Teaching
Do you remember when Jesus was in the church and someone shouted out because he was poorly? What did Jesus do?

Jesus also spoke to all the people in church and told them about God's love. Jesus had been busy all morning. Now it was nearly 12 o'clock. It was time to go and have something to eat. Jesus was staying at Capernaum with a fisherman – do you know his name? Yes, it is Simon Peter. Peter said it was now time to go home and have some food. With Peter were his brother Andrew and his friends, James and John. They were all disciples of Jesus and they were going to Simon Peter's house to eat. It was not very far to go and they were soon in the house. It was nice and cool inside but there was no food set out for them. Nothing was ready because someone in the house was poorly. Peter's mother-in-law (explain) was not very well. She was lying on a bed and had a fever that made her feel very hot. She was too ill to stand up and look after them. Perhaps they would have to go somewhere else.

Jesus was more bothered about the womann who was poorly than about eating. He could see she was not at all well and wanted to help her. He went over to her where she was lying and took hold of her hands. The hands of Jesus felt so strong and cool around her hot hands. Jesus looked at her and, still holding her hands, helped her to get up and stand on her feet. She felt better as soon as he had touched her. She was made well and wanted to do something for Jesus. She did what she was best at. She told them to sit down and she brought the food she had prepared earlier to them for to eat. Everyone in the house was amazed that Jesus had made her better just by taking her by the hand. It was a miracle.

Activity
Play 'Sleeping lions'. Pretend that you are in a deep dark jungle. You are very sleepy. While I count to ten you are to lie down and sleep. No one must move. If you move or make a noise you are out and must come and sit with me. When there is one left, go over to them, take them by the hand and say, 'Arise, for you have done well.'

Prayer
Jesus, you love people and do not want them to be ill.
We thank you for our lives and all you give to us.
Amen.

Song
Jesus' hands were kind hands

Notes

For parents and children to pray together

'Jesus, you were in Simon's house and healed his mother-in-law. Be here in our home and with us.'

Proper 2

Sunday between 10 and 16 February inclusive
(if earlier than the Second Sunday before Lent)

Aim

To show God likes us to be well and happy.

Readings

2 Kings 5:1-14
Psalm 30
1 Corinthians 9:24-27
Mark 1:40-45

Teaching

Has anyone ever been away from home in hospital? Did it make you sad that you could not be at home? At least you knew that you would get better soon and go home. A little girl was far away from her home in another country. She missed her mother and father but she was kept very busy helping in the big house. One day she noticed that the lady of the house was crying and wondered if she could help. She was told the lady's husband, Naaman, was ill and that he would not get better. He would have to leave his home and his family because he was getting worse. The little girl was sorry for Naaman and his family. All day long she wondered how she might help. Then all of a sudden she remembered a special man of God who lived in her own land. He was called Elisha and he did wonderful things with God's help. She knew what she should do: she should tell the family all about Elisha. She went to them and said, 'In my country there is a man of God called Elisha and I think he might be able to make my master Naaman better.'

They decided to go to Elisha. They had to pack bags, food, clothes, money and some gifts for God's holy man. It was a long journey but at last they arrived. Elisha had seen Naaman coming and knew why. Elisha sent a message to Naaman and this is what it said: 'Go and wash seven times in the river Jordan and you will get better.'

When Naaman heard this he was very angry. He thought Elisha would get him to do something wonderful or say some magic words. All Elisha did was tell Naaman to go and wash. Naaman said, 'There are better and cleaner rivers at home; why could he not let me go to one of them?' He was not going to do what he was asked. But his servants persuaded him by saying, 'You are lucky. The man of God has asked you to do something easy. Why not try it?'

So Naaman went down to the Jordan and dipped his feet in. Then he washed once. Was that enough? Two times, three times, let us count on our fingers, right up to seven times. He was not better after the first time, not even after six times. But after seven times God made Naaman well. Isn't God wonderful!

I am sure Naaman said a big 'thank-you' to Elisha's God and 'thank you' to Elisha. There was someone else he would have to say 'thank you' to; who was it?

Activity

Let the children play 'In the river'. Let the children make a circle around you. When you shout, 'In the river', everyone has to jump in the river. When you shout, 'On the bank', everyone has to jump backwards. This is easy. But if you shout, 'On the river' or 'In the bank', everyone must stand still. See how many can survive to jump in the river seven times.

Prayer

Father God, we thank you
for making us strong and healthy.
Keep us safe from all illness
and protect us from evil.
Amen.

Song

Thank you, Lord, for this new day

You may like to add a verse:

'Thank you, Lord, for healing us.'

Notes

Cut out and fold

Dip Naaman in the water 1, 2, 3, 4, 5, 6, 7 times.
On number 7 bring him out and show him clean.

Colour the river blue

For parents and children to pray together

'God, thank you for making us strong and happy. Protect us from illness. Amen.

Proper 3

Sunday between 17 and 23 February inclusive
(if earlier than the Second Sunday before Lent)

Aim

To show Jesus has the power to forgive and to heal.

Readings

Isaiah 43:18-25
Psalm 41
2 Corinthians 1:18-22
Mark 2:1-12

Teaching

Have you ever done anything that was naughty? Was Mummy or Daddy cross with you? When you do naughty things it makes them sad but they still love you. Jesus loves us all and wants us to be happy.

We are going to look at a house like the one Jesus was in. It has a flat roof and stairs on the outside of the house. It is a sunny country so they do not need sloping roofs. Often people would sleep on the roof or rest up there.

Look: this is the house. It is really made of wood and clay. See the steps. It would be easy to climb up them – but not if you were helping to carry someone. (Show the sequence of pictures and the roof being taken to bits. Take the lid off your house and show the hole prepared earlier.)

Look at the picture of the men lowering the paralysed man. (Be sure the children understand the man could not walk.) He needed friends to bring him to Jesus. When Jesus saw the man he was sorry for him. He said, 'Son, your sins are forgiven.' Jesus probably knew the man wanted something else. What do you think he wanted? Yes, he wanted to be made well. He wanted to walk like other people. Jesus then said to the man, 'Stand up, take your mat and go to your home.' Only Jesus could do this and he did it to make this man well again.

Activity

You will need to prepare the house before the session. Let the children make men to carry a stretcher and a man to lie on the stretcher. The stretcher could be made by one of the children. Groups of six could do a little each. Then each group could make the event happen.

Prayer

Lord Jesus, you are strong and lovely.
You want us to be healthy and happy.
Thank you for healing the man who could not walk.
Amen.

Song

These hands

Notes

Make a house from a shoe box. Remove the lid and turn the box upside down. This is the house. Put in a door, a small window and the steps. Now make a hole in the roof. After the hole is made add the lid. As the story is told let a child remove the lid.

For parents and children to pray together

'Jesus, thank you for giving us health and a good home. Thank you for our mummy and daddy who brought us to you.'

Second Sunday before Lent

Aim
To help the children to know that God loves us and made the word in which we live.

Readings
Proverbs 8:1, 22-31
Psalm 104:25-35
Colossians 1:15-20
John 1:1-14

Teaching
Look at this modelling clay. I can make things with it. Watch, I will make a cat. Now I will make something else (a human) – what is it? Yes it is a boy or a girl. Who would like to make something? (Let the children make things and say what they are.) Now I am going to take the clay away. If you do not have the clay you cannot make anything.

Once God did something very wonderful and he made it out of nothing. He had nothing to start with. He made the whole world in which we live. God the Father, Son and Holy Spirit decided to make a beautiful world. This is how it all began.

First, God made the sun, the moon and the stars. He made the sun to shine at day and the stars to shine at night. Then God made water. He made rain and rivers. He made streams and seas. What do you call a large sea? Yes, it is an ocean. Then God made the land – or we would all have had to be fish! He made hills and mountains, valleys and beaches and he made them all out of his love. He thought, 'How lovely.'

Then he made grass, trees and flowers and all growing things. Tell me some of the things that God made. He made all these out of his love. He saw that they were lovely.

Then in the waters God made fish; in the air he made birds, large ones and small ones; on the land he made animals. Tell me the names of some. God loved all that he made and thought they were lovely.

After he made the world, God decided it was now time to make people. God wanted someone who would love him because he loved everything. He wanted someone who would love the world like he loved the world. So he made the first man and called him Adam. Then, because God knew Adam would like someone to share the world with, he made a woman and called her Eve. They would love each other as God loved them. They would learn to love the world like God loved the world. And God made all of this out of his own love.

Activity
Have pictures of beautiful things for the children to stick on a frieze. Let them also draw something they love and add it to the frieze and write their name against it. Have in big letters underneath: GOD MADE ALL OF THESE.

Prayer
God, Father, Son and Holy Spirit,
thank you for the lovely world, which you made.
As we look at the world and at ourselves
help us to know you made us out of your love.
Amen.

Song
God who made the earth

Notes

God made them all

For parents and children to pray together

'God, thank you for a wonderful world and for all that is in it. Thank you for giving us life.'

Sunday before Lent

Aim
To show that Jesus brings light to our lives.

Readings
2 Kings 2:1-12
Psalm 50:1-6
2 Corinthians 4:3-6
Mark 9:2-9

Teaching
When it gets dark what do you do? Yes, you put on a light and the darkness disappears. Streetlights make our towns and villages safer. If we have to go down a dark street, we take a torch with us so that we can see more clearly in the dark. Perhaps at home you have a light that is left on all night or a light that comes on when it is dark. (Let the children talk about different lights.)

What is the brightest light we have ever seen? Yes, it is the sun. But no one can look at the sun because it is too bright. It can hurt our eyes by its brightness and can even make us go blind. We should never look directly at the sun. The sun gives the world light and life but we cannot look directly at it.

When Jesus went up a mountain with Peter, James and John it was to show them who he really is, to let them see he is the Light of the World. High up in the mountain, when they were away from everyone else and very quiet, Jesus said his prayers. While he was praying the three disciples saw his clothes glowing bright and white. They were amazed at the brightness. Then from a cloud they heard a voice – it was the voice of God. God actually spoke to them and said to them, 'This is my Son, my loved one; listen to him.' The disciples looked around to see who spoke but they could see no one, only Jesus. God was behind the cloud because he was too wonderful for the disciples to look at; he protected them from his brightness by the cloud. When they were going down the mountain they thought they would like to tell everybody what had happened, but Jesus said, 'Do not tell anyone just now; keep it a secret.' We are lucky because we know that secret. We know Jesus is God's Son and he is the Light of the World.

Activity
Play musical statues. Every time the music stops shine a light around, aiming at the feet of the children. Anyone who moves or cannot be quiet is out. This is more effective if it can be done in a semi-dark room.

Prayer
Jesus, we know you are the Light of the World.
Shine in our lives
and make them bright and beautiful.
Amen.

Song
God who made the earth.

Notes

Jesus on the Mountain with Peter, James and John

For parents and children to pray together

'Jesus, you are the Light of the World,
shine in our homes and in our lives
making them bright and beautiful!'

LENT
First Sunday of Lent

Aim
To show God's love for the world.

Readings
Genesis 9:8-17
Psalm 25:1-10
1 Peter 3:18-22
Mark 1:9-15

Teaching
Show the children a wooden Noah's Ark or a picture. Tell them about Noah and the animals going into the Ark and how God was sending rain on the world because the people were doing bad things. The rains came down and the floods came up (make sure the children know what a flood is). Repeat 'The rains came down' and make actions with your hands. 'The floods came up', make actions with your hands. The floods covered the streets, the houses, the trees, the hills, the mountains and the whole earth. As you list these (and anything else the children can think of that would be covered by the floods), say and act out, 'The rains came down and the floods came up' after each suggestion.

Water covered all the earth but Noah, his family and all the animals were safe. Why? Because, they were in the ark. When the rain stopped they could not leave the ark for there was very deep water everywhere. After a long time, Noah sent out a big black bird called a raven to see if there was dry land and it did not come back. It flew round and round until it could find dry land in the mountains. Noah then sent out another bird, a dove, but it came back because there was still too much water. After a week he sent it out again. When it came back it had a branch in its beak. Noah knew the waters had gone down. After another week he sent out the dove again and it did not come back – the floods had gone away. The first thing Noah did was to get out of the ark and say 'Thank you' to God for keeping them safe. God told Noah to look up at the sky. Noah looked up and the sky was full of beautiful colours. It was a rainbow. Has anyone seen a rainbow? (Show a picture of a rainbow.)

God promised that such a big flood would not cover the earth again. God put the rainbow in the sky to remind us that God loves the world and God loves you and me.

Activity
Use a wooden model of Noah's Ark for the story. Give each pair of children a piece of coloured wool (about 50 centimetres), making sure they know the name of the colour. Have all the colours of the rainbow. When you call out a colour the children with that colour form an arch and the rest then pass underneath the arch. Sometimes call out three or four colours to make arches and let the rest pass through. Finally call out all the colours and let the rainbow be made. You could try to pass under it. (A reminder of the colours: red, orange, yellow, green, blue, indigo and violet.)

Give each child strands from all the colours and ask them to make a rainbow by sticking them on the template provided.

Prayer
God, we thank you for the colours of the rainbow
and for showing your love for the world
in the sun and the rain.
Amen.

Song
Read or sing verses of 'Mister Noah built an ark'. Teach the children the two refrains.

Notes

God loves the world. God loves me.

For parents and children to pray together

'God, thank you for the sunshine and rain. Thank you for your love and care. We give our love to you.'

Second Sunday of Lent

Aim

To encourage the children to be generous.

Readings

Genesis 17:1-7, 15-16
Psalm 22:23-31
Romans 4:13-25
Mark 8:31-38

Teaching

Once upon a time there was a beggar who sat by the roadside. He was near the market and begged for food. Most of the farmers who came to the market gave him a few of their seeds. The beggar put these in a sack behind his back, so that no one could see it. Then he could beg for some more. One day a prince came along and the beggar shouted for help. He had a lot in his sack but he thought the prince would give him something special. The prince came to him and said, 'You give me something first.' The beggar put his hand around the back and took a handful of grain. But he let it trickle through his fingers and brought out one single tiny grain. For a moment the prince took the grain in his hand and then gave it back to the beggar. The grain was changed into a tiny piece of gold. Now the beggar was sad that he had been so greedy. If he had given the whole sack to the prince, just think what the prince might have done with it.

Jesus wants us to give him some of our time in prayer. He wants us to give him our love and our friendship. How can we do that? We can say our prayers every day. We can try and be good and kind. We can be generous and not greedy. Listen to this story of someone who gave all that she had to God (Mark 12:41-44).

There was a poor woman who had very little of anything but she wanted to give something to God. She wanted to go to the Temple church and give God something that was special to her. She looked around the house but she did not have anything that she could give. All that she had was two tiny coins – it was all the money she had. She could not really spare it but she wanted to be generous and to give it to God. Off she went to the Temple to put it in the big money box at the church. As she went she saw rich men carrying purses full of money. They dropped their money into the box bit by bit, making as much noise with it as they could. She waited until she thought no one was watching and she came forward and dropped her two tiny coins in the box. They did not make a sound. Then she went away thinking no one would have noticed but it did not matter because God knew she had given a gift. What she did not know was that Jesus also saw her and he said to his disciples, 'This poor woman has given more than the others. For the others had put in what they had to spare but she has given all that she had.'

Activity

Get the children to act out the two stories. Let some be generous farmers who give grain. You could use rice or any other grain, giving them a small handful each. Let the beggar hide it all in a bag. Make sure all see the beggar give only one tiny grain and then go off sadly with a bagful.

Have a box or tin for the children to drop coins in, making a noise. Let the poor woman's coins be tiny. Make sure they all understand how generous she is.

Prayer

God, we love you
for you have given us life and many good things.
Help us to be kind and willing to share with others.
Amen.

Song

Two little fishes, five loaves of bread

Notes

She gave all that she had.

Who gives little can only receive little.

For parents and children to pray together

'God, thank you for our food and our homes. Help us to be kind to all in need.'

Third Sunday of Lent

Aim

To help the children understand we are called to love God and each other.

Readings

Exodus 20:1-17
Psalm 19
1 Corinthians 1:18-25
John 2:13-22

Teaching

Moses loved God and wanted to do what God wanted him to do. He was the leader of a lot of people and he was taking them through the desert. (Who knows what a desert is? Explain.) For a long time they lived in the desert and they wanted to do what God wanted them to do. Moses went up a mountain called Sinai. (Does anyone know what a mountain is?) Moses climbed high up the mountain until he was out of sight. The mountain was wrapped in fire and smoke because God was on the mountain waiting to meet Moses. There was a loud noise like the sound of a trumpet. Moses was not full of fear because he was meeting with God. God wanted to tell Moses what he wanted the people to do. God wanted the people to love him and to love each other. To help them, God gave Moses some rules about what they could do.

The rules were called 'The Ten Commandments'. (Let us count to ten.) There were four commandments which said we had to love God more than anything else and six which told us we had to love other people also. (Four and six: who knows how many that makes?) There were four which told us to love God, one that told us to love our parents, and five that told us to love other people. (4+1+5 = ?) Let us count again to ten. Some people find it hard to remember ten different things so Jesus told us how the Ten Commandments could be remembered as two. Listen, this is what Jesus said: 'You shall love the Lord your God with all your heart, and with all your soul, and with all your mind. This is the greatest and the first commandment. And the second is like it: You shall love your neighbour as yourself.' (Let someone read these verses out to the class.) What do you think Jesus was saying we should do? Yes, it sounds quite simple: we should love God and love each other. (Let the group talk about how we can do this). Let's look at our paper and read the words together:

LOVE GOD
LOVE OTHERS

God wants us to keep a special place for him in our hearts. He wants to know that we love him. We can show our love by talking to him each day in prayer and by doing what he wants us to do. God wants a place in our love and in our lives.

We can show our love to our parents by doing what they ask us to do and saying how we love them. We can show our love to others by being kind and generous. We are asked to LOVE GOD and LOVE OTHERS.

Activity

Play 'Musical chairs'. Have one chair on which there is a notice saying, 'Reserved', and tell the children that no one can sit in that chair as it is being kept for someone special. When the game is over sit in the reserved chair and say, 'I am lucky for this was kept for me.'

Prayer

God, you love us.
God, we love you.
We love our parents.
Help us to love each other.
Amen.

Song

Two little eyes

Notes

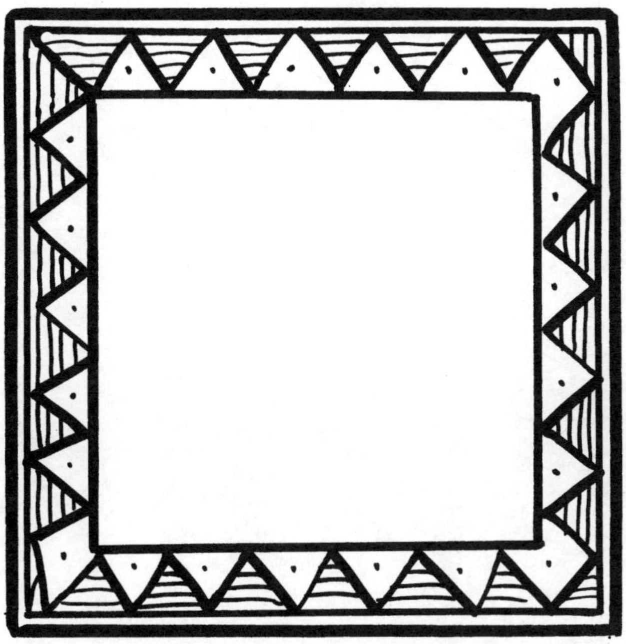

Draw a picture of someone who loves you

God loves

_ _ _ _ _ _ _ _ _ _

write your name

and wants me to love everyone

For parents and children to pray together

'God, thank you for loving us all. Thank you for all the love we share with each other. We all love you.

Fourth Sunday of Lent
Mothering Sunday

Today is a day for the family to worship together, to rejoice in being a family and to give thanks for their mutual love. Involve as many of the children as possible in doing things. Let them bring up the bread and the wine, and take the collection. The children may carry banners expressing thanksgiving for the love of their homes and the love of God. Children could be encouraged to bring a photograph of their mother with them when they come to the altar rail. Let the young people lead some of the intercessions and some of the readings. A mother and a child could share in a reading. If flowers or cards are given out, remember that all of us have a mother. Encourage all to come forward. Some may then like to place their flowers or card near the candles if their mother has died and is now in God's kingdom and love.

Notes

Happy Mother's Day
I love you
Thank you

For parents and children to pray together
'God, thank you for our home: for all the love that is in it. Thank you, especially today, for our mothers.'

Fifth Sunday of Lent

Aim

To look towards the crucifixion and resurrection.

Readings

Jeremiah 31:31-34
Psalm 51:1-12 or Psalm 119:9-16
Hebrews 5:5-10
John 12:20-33

Teaching

Has anyone ever planted seeds or bulbs? What did you do? You buried them in the soil. You covered them over and then waited until they grew. If you did not bury the seeds, but kept them in a packet in your house, what would happen to them? Nothing.

Go over the story of Lazy Jack. Have him look at the seed and admire it but not plant it. Have him keep the seed 'safe'. In doing this there was no growth and the harvest was lost. If seeds are to grow, they have to be planted in the ground.

Jesus told his disciples that what was going to happen to him was like planting seeds in the ground. He would die on the cross. He would be buried. But like seeds he would rise again. Let us think of the days when this happened. Jesus died on a Friday. Does anyone know what it is called? It is called Good Friday. On that day Jesus was on the cross. (Show a crucifix or a picture of the crucifixion and talk about it.) On Good Friday Jesus died and was buried – just like seeds are buried in the earth. On the Saturday nothing happened. Then on the Sunday Jesus rose again – he was alive and seen by his friends. Does anyone know what we call the day Jesus rose again? It is called Easter Day. It is the day we get Easter Eggs and are glad that Jesus is alive. It will soon be Easter and we will say, 'Thank you' to God that Jesus is alive. We will plant some seeds in a box and see if they can grow by Easter.

Activity

Have a seed tray full of seed compost and a packet of cress or some other quickly germinating seed. You may like to mark out a seed planting area in the shape of a cross. Give the children two or three tiny seeds each (with spares for those who lose them). It is better to give a child the seeds when it is their turn to plant them and to direct them in the planting. Do not forget to water the seeds and keep them in a warm place. After the seed is planted the children can sing and act out:

> This is the way we plant our seeds,
> plant our seeds, plant our seeds.
> This is the way we plant our seeds
> on a Sunday morning.
>
> This is the way the seeds do sleep,
> seeds do sleep, seeds do sleep.
> This is the way the seeds do sleep
> on a Sunday morning.
>
> This is the way they rise again,
> rise again, rise again.
> This is the way they rise again
> on a Sunday morning.
>
> (Tune: 'Here we go round the mulberry bush')

First verse: bend down, sowing seeds in the ground.
Second verse: curl up on the ground.
Third verse: jump up and wave your hands.

Prayer

God, we thank you for all things that grow;
that buried seeds rise again.
We thank you for the love of Jesus.
Amen.

Song

Jesus' love is very wonderful

Notes

For parents and children to pray together

'God, we thank you for seeds and for all things that live and grow.'

Palm Sunday

Aim

To enjoy the triumphal entry into Jerusalem.

Readings

Liturgy of the Palms
Mark 11:1-11 or John 12:12-16
Psalm 118: 1, 2, 19-29

Liturgy of the Passion
Isaiah 50:4-9a
Psalm 31:9-16
Philippians 2:5-11
Mark 14:1–15:47 or Mark 15:1-39 (40-47)

Let the dramatic readings of the Passion narratives replace the sermon today. Allow the Scriptures to speak for themselves. Use as many people as possible to share in the readings. I have provided ideas for the Liturgy of the Palms rather than comment on the Passion: I hope Holy Week will be used to do that.

Teaching

If someone important comes to where you live, people usually crowd the streets to see them. (Ask the children for examples – athletes and sports people, the Queen, a pop star.) They often come in special cars or buses. This is a story of Jesus when he came to Jerusalem riding on a donkey. Has anyone ever had a ride on a donkey?

There was once a young donkey that lived with its mother. No one had ever been on its back. It would run and kick its heels and then go back to its mother and snuggle up close.

The donkey had a kind master. His master loved to hear Jesus talk and tell people about the love of God.

The little donkey dreamt that one day someone would ride upon him as they did on his mother. One day, two strangers came and started to unloose him from where he was tied with his mother. 'I wonder what they want?' thought the donkey. Someone was going to stop them but they were told, 'The Master needs him.' And they let the donkey go. The little donkey was going to carry the Lord Jesus. He felt so proud as he was led away. When he got to where Jesus was, people were so excited. Some people took off their coats and put them on the donkey to make a soft seat for Jesus. At first the donkey was surprised when Jesus got on his back – he had never carried anyone before – but soon he found it exciting. It was wonderful because people spread their cloaks on the ground for the donkey to walk on. This did not usually happen to donkeys but Jesus was a special person.

People started to wave and cheer. They cut down palm branches and laid them for the donkey to walk on. They shouted, 'Hosanna!' (Let us shout it again, but this time shout a little louder. Now let us shout it three times.) 'Hosanna' means 'Save us now'. (Sing the chorus from 'Give me joy in my heart'.) The people shouted and sang to Jesus because they thought he had come as their king. They did not understand Jesus wanted to be king of peace and to rule in their hearts.

People crowded around as Jesus entered Jerusalem. The little donkey knew it was doing something very important for it was carrying Jesus.

Activity

Show the children the donkey on the worksheet. Let them put Jesus on the donkey and then colour them in. Use glue to fix Jesus on the donkey.

Prayer

Dear Jesus, we want to sing songs of Hosanna to you.
We are so glad you rode into Jerusalem on a donkey.
We would like to help you do your work.
Amen.

Song

Give me joy in my heart

Notes

Make a palm tree - useful for waving in church
cut about 8cm into paper and 2.5cm apart
Use A4 paper - green if possible or colour it
Roll tightly and stick where shaded
Gently pull out the branches

Sit Jesus on the donkey
Colour me in and give me a tail

EASTER
Easter Day

Aim
To experience the joy of the resurrection.

Readings
Acts 10:34-43 or Isaiah 25:6-9
Psalm 118:1, 2, 14-24
1 Corinthians 15:1-11 or Acts 10:34-43
John 20:1-18 or Mark 16:1-8

Teaching
Look at the Easter garden, beginning with the stone rolled against the tomb. Make sure they know who was buried there on Good Friday. (Get them to repeat, 'Good Friday.') Tell how no one would go there on the Sabbath day. Now it was Easter Day and Mary wanted to go to be near the body of Jesus. If the church has figures of Jesus and Mary, show Mary, or you may be able to show her from an Easter card. Mary wondered who could move the stone. It was big and heavy; it would take a few men to move it. We know that before she got there the stone was rolled away. (Let a child roll the stone gently aside.) Mary looked for Jesus but could not find his body. Mary was very sad. Mary was crying. (Let the children repeat, 'Mary was crying.') She went and told Peter and John, and they came and looked into the tomb but saw no one. They went away and Mary came back. Mary was crying. (Get all to repeat.)

She thought she heard someone coming along the path. Perhaps it was the gardener. She would ask him if he knew where the body of Jesus was. 'I am looking for Jesus and I cannot find him. Do you know where they have taken him?'

Then she heard a voice she knew saying her name, 'Mary, Mary.'

There was only one person who could say her name like that. Who is it? Yes, Jesus, and he is alive. Repeat after me: 'Jesus is alive.' At this point show the figure or a picture of Jesus. Let all look at it and make comments. Jesus is not a ghost: he is alive.

Then Jesus told Mary, 'You must go and tell the disciples you have seen me and that I am alive.' Mary did not want to leave Jesus but she did as he asked her. She went and said to the disciples, 'I have seen the Lord.' Let us say what Mary said: 'I have seen the Lord.'

Activity
If possible, all the children should take part in the activities in church. You may like to have an Easter-egg painting competition or a miniature Easter-garden competition. Eggs could be brought hard-boiled and decorated during their class if you have one. An Easter-egg hunt is always fun, especially if it can be outside. You could have an egg-rolling competition or even and egg 'jarping' contest (this is a little like conkers: the children clash eggs and see which break first). Easter cards to take home could be made.

If the story is told, get the children to mime it. Let half the children be Mary and the other half Jesus. You could keep a few to be the disciples.

Prayer
Let us all say, 'God, we thank you that Jesus is alive and loves us. Alleluia.'

(You may like to help them to sing 'Alleluia'.)

Song
This is the day

(Let a leader or a group sing it in parts and the children repeat the same words.)

Notes

Jesus is risen

Colour in the egg with felt tips.

For parents and children to pray together

Jesus, you died on the cross
(make the shape with your arms)

Jesus, you were buried
(curl up on the ground)

Jesus, you rose again
(jump up and shout)
'Alleluia!'

Second Sunday of Easter

Aim

To share in the resurrection joy of the disciples.

Readings

Acts 4:32-35
Psalm 133
1 John 1:1–2:2
John 20:19-31

Teaching

Show some keys on a bunch and let the children guess what they might be for. Have a variety of keys: a large key, a yale or chubb lock key and a tiny key. Establish that keys are for locking and unlocking. Ask for suggestions why places should be locked or unlocked.

The disciples locked themselves in a room. Do you know why? They were afraid after Jesus was killed that the same people might come looking for them. So the disciples were hiding in a house with a locked door – no one could get in. They were talking very quietly. Suddenly Jesus was there with them. He was alive and said, 'Shalom'; that means 'Hello' or 'Peace be with you'. Jesus was saying, 'Hello, I am back.' Mary said he was alive and that she had seen him in the garden. Now there he was in the room. Strange, because no one had unlocked the door but Jesus was there inside. He suddenly appeared. He was not a ghost – he was really alive again. The disciples were really pleased to see him. They would have liked to ask all sorts of questions. Jesus had some work for them to do. He wanted them to tell others that he was alive. He wanted them to do the work he had been doing. To help them he came to each one of them and breathed his Spirit into them. The ten disciples were really glad to see Jesus. Why was there just ten? There should have been twelve. Do you know who was missing? Judas was missing because he had died. Thomas was also missing because he had gone away. When Thomas came back he was sorry that he had missed Jesus. The disciples said, 'We have seen the Lord.' (Let us repeat: 'We have seen the Lord.') Thomas said, 'I cannot believe that he is alive; I saw him die. I will only believe if I see him, if I can touch him. I would like to feel the nail holes in his hands and put my hand in his side where the spear made a hole. Then I will believe.'

It was a week after Easter and Jesus came again to where the disciples were. This time Thomas was with them. Jesus spoke to Thomas and said, 'Thomas, come here – put your finger in the nail holes, put your hand where the spear has been.' Thomas did not know what to do. He came before Jesus and touched his hands and his side and said quietly, 'My Lord and my God.' (Let us repeat: 'My Lord and my God.')

Now all of the disciples had seen Jesus. How many were there who saw him?

Let us say what they said: 'We have seen the Lord.'

Let us say what Mary Magdalene said: 'I have seen the Lord.'

They all knew that Jesus who had been dead was alive again and wanted to be their friend.

Activity

Tell the children that one is to be blindfolded and placed in the middle of a circle. The others sitting in a circle will pass the keys around. At a command they will stop and the person with the keys hides them behind their back. Everyone puts their hands behind their back. Now the blindfold is removed and the person in the middle has three chances to guess who has the keys. To help, the person with the keys should give them a gentle shake (especially when the person in the middle is looking away). If they guess correctly, the person with the keys should go into the middle and the game begins again.

Prayer

Jesus, we are glad that you are alive
and that you want to be our friend.
Let us remember you every day
and speak to you in our prayers.
Amen.

Song

Sing verse 3 of 'Away in a manger' and relate it to the resurrection.

Notes

The disciples were glad to see Jesus

For parents and children to pray together

'Lord Jesus,
you are alive
and want to be friends.
We welcome you into our home.'

Third Sunday of Easter

Aim

To encourage the children to know Jesus as their friend.

Readings

Acts 3:12-19
Psalm 4
1 John 3:1-7
Luke 24:36-48

Teaching

Once there was a little boy who was going to walk home from school in the dark. It was a long way and the teacher was worried that he might be frightened. He said he was not. Just before he went home the teacher again asked him because she was worried about him walking in the dark. The boy again said he was not frightened because he had a big torch and it had a lovely light. After this he said he was not worried for he would not be alone as his father would be outside waiting for him.

What makes you frightened? Encourage the children to talk of fears – and to see it is sometimes good to have fears.

After Jesus died, the disciples were frightened that they might be captured, so they hid. They locked themselves in, so that no one would find them. They did not dare go out. Then Jesus came. At first they were frightened of Jesus. Do you know why? They thought Jesus was a ghost. But he was not. He came to them as their friend to help them not to be afraid. He had to show them he was not a ghost. He let them touch him, feel the nail holes in his feet and hands. Then he asked for something to eat; they knew that ghosts did not eat.

Jesus came to be their friend and to give them courage. He asked them to go out and to tell people that he was alive. He promised that he would go with them, so that they were not alone. They could talk to him and get strength from him.

Jesus wants us to be his friend. He wants us to know he is with us and that we can talk to him. He wants us to tell other people that he is alive and will be their friend.

Activity

This is a variation on 'What time is it, Mr Wolf?' Choose one person to be 'Spook'. As Spook walks away, the children follow behind asking the time. Spook can say any time he likes leading the children further away. When he says, 'Midnight', he turns, chasing the children and crying, 'Whoo, whoo, whoo'. The first person caught or the last back to base is the next Spook.

Prayer

Jesus, friend of the disciples,
be a friend of mine.
Let me know that you love me and you are with me.
Let me learn to talk to you every day.
Amen.

Song

Jesus, we thank you

Notes

Draw the boy's father and a light in the boy's hand

Draw around Jesus who came to his disciples

Jesus says, 'Do not be afraid. I am with you.'

For parents and children to pray together

'Jesus, risen and alive.
We love you.
Thank you for being with us.'

Fourth Sunday of Easter

Aim

To show how Jesus, the Good Shepherd, loves us.

Readings

Acts 4:5-12
Psalm 23
1 John 3:16-24
John 10:11-18

Teaching

Have you ever lost anything that you really cared for? Perhaps you lost a favourite toy? Do you remember how you looked and looked for it until you found it? Were you not really glad when you found it? (Let the children talk about lost things.)

Now, has anyone here ever been lost? It is horrible to be lost and it makes you sad and afraid. But Mummy and Daddy would look for you – other people might help. Sometimes people wander away from God and get lost but he will seek and seek until he finds them. He will not give up because he loves them.

Jesus said that he is a shepherd caring for his sheep. He is a good shepherd because he loves his sheep and will risk his life for any that are lost.

Let us think of a little sheep that has gone astray. It has wandered from its mother and gone to where it is dangerous. Soon it will get dark and the wolf will come looking for the lamb and if it catches the lamb, it will gobble it all up. The little lamb does not know which way to go. It cries (let the children make lamb sounds) The wolf pricks up his ears; he hears a cry and it sounds like his supper. The lamb cries again (let the children cry). The wolf licks its lips. But this time the shepherd heard the lamb and started to move quickly towards it. The wolf was also moving. Suddenly the shepherd called the little lamb by its name. This time it cried out with joy (let he children still make lamb sounds). The shepherd ran and rescued the lamb just in time. He picked it up, put it around the back his neck and carried it home safely. Everyone was so happy when the little lamb was safe. The shepherd did this because he loves his sheep. Jesus loves us and seeks us if we are lost. He rescues us from danger and brings us to safety. This is why we sometimes call Jesus the Good Shepherd. Let us all say, 'Jesus is the Good Shepherd.'

Activity

Play 'What time is it, Mr Wolf?'

Mr Wolf is chosen and walks away with the rest following. Now you say loudly, 'What time is it, Mr Wolf?' Mr Wolf can say any time he likes as he leads the children further from the fold. When he answers, 'Twelve o'clock – dinner time', all must run back to the fold, making the sound of sheep. Mr Wolf runs after them. The person he catches is the next Mr Wolf.

Prayer

Jesus, you are the Good Shepherd;
you love us all
and seek all who are lost or in trouble.
May we learn to follow you
and to love you all our days.
Amen.

Song

Little lamb has lost its way,
lost its way,
lost its way.
Little lamb has lost its way.
Let the shepherd find it.

Little child has lost its way,
lost its way,
lost its way.
Little child has lost its way.
Good Shepherd, find it.

(Tune: 'London Bridge is falling down')

Notes

Help the shepherd find his sheep

for parents and children to pray together

'Jesus, you love us
and care if we
are lost. You are
our Good Shepherd.
Thank you.'

write your name on the sheep

Fifth Sunday of Easter

Aim

To help the children to share and pass on Good News.

Readings

Acts 8:26-40
Psalm 22:25-31
1 John 4:7-21
John 15:1-8

Teaching

Show a bunch of grapes and ask if they know what sort of plant they come from. Vines grow lots of grapes and because of this we can buy them in our shops. How do you think grapes are grown? What do they need to grow?

The vine needs to be planted. It needs soil. It needs sun. It needs rain. (If it is in a greenhouse, it will need someone to water it.) It needs someone to care for it if it is to grow well.

These grapes have been well looked after: they have grown beautifully. Because they have had proper sun and rain they taste lovely. Who would like one? Let us share them. Let everyone have one. Who would like to give them out? (Let two children go around the class giving out a grape or two if there are plenty.)

The grapes were mine – but I like sharing. I like sharing the stories of Jesus and his disciples. It is a pity when people are greedy or keep good things to themselves. Jesus wants us to grow in what we believe and to share with others. We grow:

by coming to our class,
by saying our prayers,
by showing our love for God,
by doing what God wants,
by caring for the world,
by having someone to care for us.

Activity

Hide paper vine leaves around the room. Ask the class to find them. Let there be only one for each child. Anyone who finds two must give them both away and look for or receive another. Let this go on until everyone has a leaf. Have on the vine leaves simple words: 'Jesus', 'God', 'Love', 'Pray', 'Care', 'Share'. Help the children to read them and see if they can say what they mean. The leaves can be coloured green.

Prayer

Jesus, you shared your life with us,
you gave us your love.
We love you and want to share with you.
Amen.

Song

Lord of the loving heart

Notes

Can you find the name JESUS?

How many leaves?

How many bunches of grapes?

How many disciples did Jesus have?

For parents and children to pray together

'Jesus, help us to work with you. Let us grow more like you in all we say and do. We love you.'

Sixth Sunday of Easter

Aim
To encourage the children to see Jesus as a friend.

Readings
Acts 10:44-48
Psalm 98
1 John 5:1-6
John 15:9-17

Teaching
Do you know what a slave is? A slave is someone who always has to do what they are told. They do not share in the good things. Sometimes they are fastened by chains; they are not free to go out or in when they want. They cannot share in the riches of the master. Sometimes the master can be cruel to them. (Maybe the children know a story of a wicked king.)

Cinderella was a sort of slave to the ugly sisters. They made her do all the horrible jobs and were unkind to her. Cinderella was rather sad and not allowed to do nice things. (Tell the story briefly.)

Jesus wants us to be his friends. He does not want us to be servants or slaves. He wants us to work with him and to enjoy being with him. Let us all choose a friend in the room. (Get the children to join up in pairs.) How do we keep our friends? By talking to them and by sharing with them. I am now going to give one of each pair a picture to colour and I will give to the other one the felt tips or crayons. No one will be able to do the work unless we share with our friend. Let us share the pictures and the colours. Let us say which colours we would like to use and share with each other. Let us work as friends.

To be a friend of Jesus we need to learn to talk to him every day. What do you call talking to Jesus? Yes we call it 'praying' or 'saying our prayers'. Let us all say the prayer on our sheet. I will say it first and then you can say it after me, line by line.

Activity
'Do as I say.' Everyone faces the leader and must do what the leader tells them. They must not follow the actions of the leader if these are different. When the leader says, 'Touch your nose', they all touch their noses. If the leader says, 'Stand up', they all stand up. If the leader says, 'Sit down', they all sit down. If the leader says, 'Stand still', and then jumps, any who jump are out. If the leader says, 'Raise one arm', whilst lifting two, anyone who raises two arms is out.

Prayer
Jesus, friend of little children,
be a friend to me.
Let me learn to love you
and know you are with me.
Jesus, be with me always
as a friend and a helper.
Amen.

Song
Jesus is a friend of mine

Notes

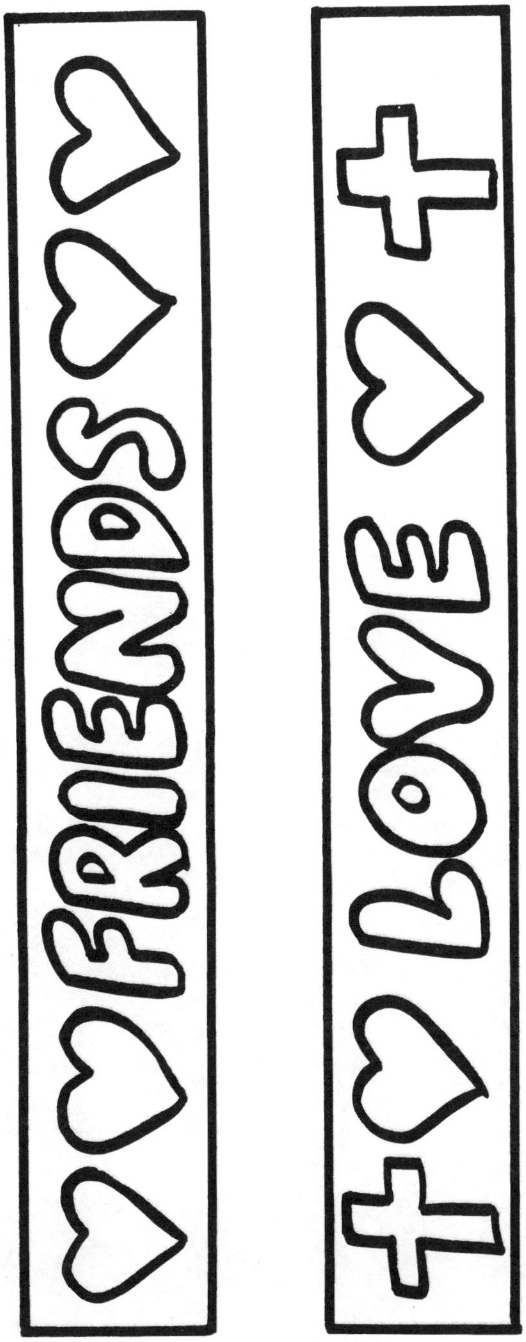

Secure the bracelets with a paperclip.

Once both bracelets are made, let the children exchange them with each other.

For parents and children to pray together

'Jesus, we thank you for all our friends and all who love us. We are glad that you love us and are our friend.'

Ascension Day

As this is a working day and a school day, I have assumed there will be no separate teaching for the children and young people. However, I feel, if the opportunity is there, the children should be encouraged to go up into the church tower or a high place and release balloons with tags on them celebrating the Ascension. I have included suggestions for tags and banners that could be made during the sermon if the young people have the opportunity to withdraw. I have also included a hymn for each group. This is an important event and if missed on Ascension Day the material could be used on the Sunday following.

Song

I'm singing your praise, Lord

Notes

Jesus on high
loves us

Jesus is
our friend

I love
Jesus

Seventh Sunday of Easter

Aim
To show that Jesus is always present and working with his disciples.

Readings
Acts 1:15-17, 21-26
Psalm 1
1 John 5:9-13
John 17:6-19

Teaching
Some days when there is a lot of cloud we cannot see the sun shining. Where has the sun gone? Yes, it is there behind the cloud. It has not gone away; it is just hidden. Sometimes you can tell the sun is behind the clouds because the cloud has a silver lining or rays of light escape from behind the cloud. Even when it is very cloudy we know the sun has not gone away. Tell the Ascension story. Help the children to understand that Jesus had not gone away; rather, he is hidden from our sight but always there. Let the children visualise the cloud that hid Jesus. Tell them how the same cloud was hiding the Father from the eyes of the disciples. Jesus and the Father are hidden from us but they are here. Remind them of the last words of Jesus as he was hidden: 'Remember, I am with you always' (Matthew 28:20).

Let the children colour the cloud on the worksheet. Encourage them to make the cloud dark and to add a silver lining.

The disciples watched Jesus enter into the cloud. Then they went back to Jerusalem. They kept thinking about the last words Jesus said to them. When we leave someone what do we usually say? 'Ta-ta', 'Goodbye', 'See you soon', 'Cheerio'. Jesus did not say goodbye because he was not leaving his disciples. They would not be able to see him but he was with them. They learnt they could still talk to him and he would still help them. Jesus is with us and he wants us to talk to him.

Activity
If the space allows, play hide-and-seek. If this is not possible, hide a few small articles before the children arrive and ask them to find them. You could tape things to the underside of seats or to curtains. Encourage them to know there are lots of things hidden and they will only be found if we look for them.

Help them to trace around the words 'I am with you always'. Tell them this is what Jesus says to us.

Prayer
Jesus, you are with us always.
We come to give our love to you
and we want to be your friends.
We cannot see you but we still love you.
Amen.

Song
Come on and shine

Notes

I am with you always

Cut out cloud and feed through slits to hide Jesus

Pentecost

Aim

To celebrate the power of the Spirit.

Readings

Acts 2:1-21 or Ezekiel 37:1-14
Psalm 104:24-34, 35b
Romans 8:22-27 or Acts 2:1-21
John 15:26-27; 16:4b-15

Teaching

Have some toys that need batteries or power packs. A car that can be controlled would be ideal. Show the children the toys without their batteries and ask if they know what is wrong with them. Why do they lack power? Get the children to push them and see how they still do not go properly. Now produce the source of power. If they can, let the children snap on power packs or add batteries. Will this make a difference? Let the children see the difference it makes. If necessary, remove the batteries and replace them again to emphasise the difference they make.

The twelve disciples had been asked to tell the world about Jesus. They were to be strong and brave and not be afraid, but they did not have the power to do this by themselves. Jesus told them to wait in Jerusalem until the power of the Spirit was given to them, to wait until they were given power from God. At Pentecost they were waiting in a room in Jerusalem when there was a powerful sound like a big wind. (Let us make a sound like the wind.) It was a really big sound. (Let us make a bigger sound.) The sound was heard because the Spirit of God had come to give the disciples power. The wind, which was the Spirit of God, filled the whole house where they were. The power of God had come and was filling the disciples.

Then on each of the twelve disciples there was what looked like flames of fire. It did not burn them because it was really the Spirit of God. Over the head of each disciple were these wonderful flames.

Now the disciples were given power from the Spirit of God. They were made brave and strong. They were not afraid any more. They knew God was with them. Now they would go out in power and tell the people about Jesus.

Activity

Let the children play with the toys that have batteries and power packs. Show the children how they work and how they need to be switched on. Tell them how power goes from the batteries to the toys and how the toys will not work properly without this power.

Make paper hats of flames of fire that can be worn for the end of the service if the children return to church.

Prayer

Holy Spirit, come to us.
Fill us with your power.
Help us to be strong.
Help us to be brave,
and to know you are with us.
Amen.

Song

I'm a pow, pow, powerpack

Notes

Colour hat of flames.
Punch holes once folded.
Use wool to fasten.

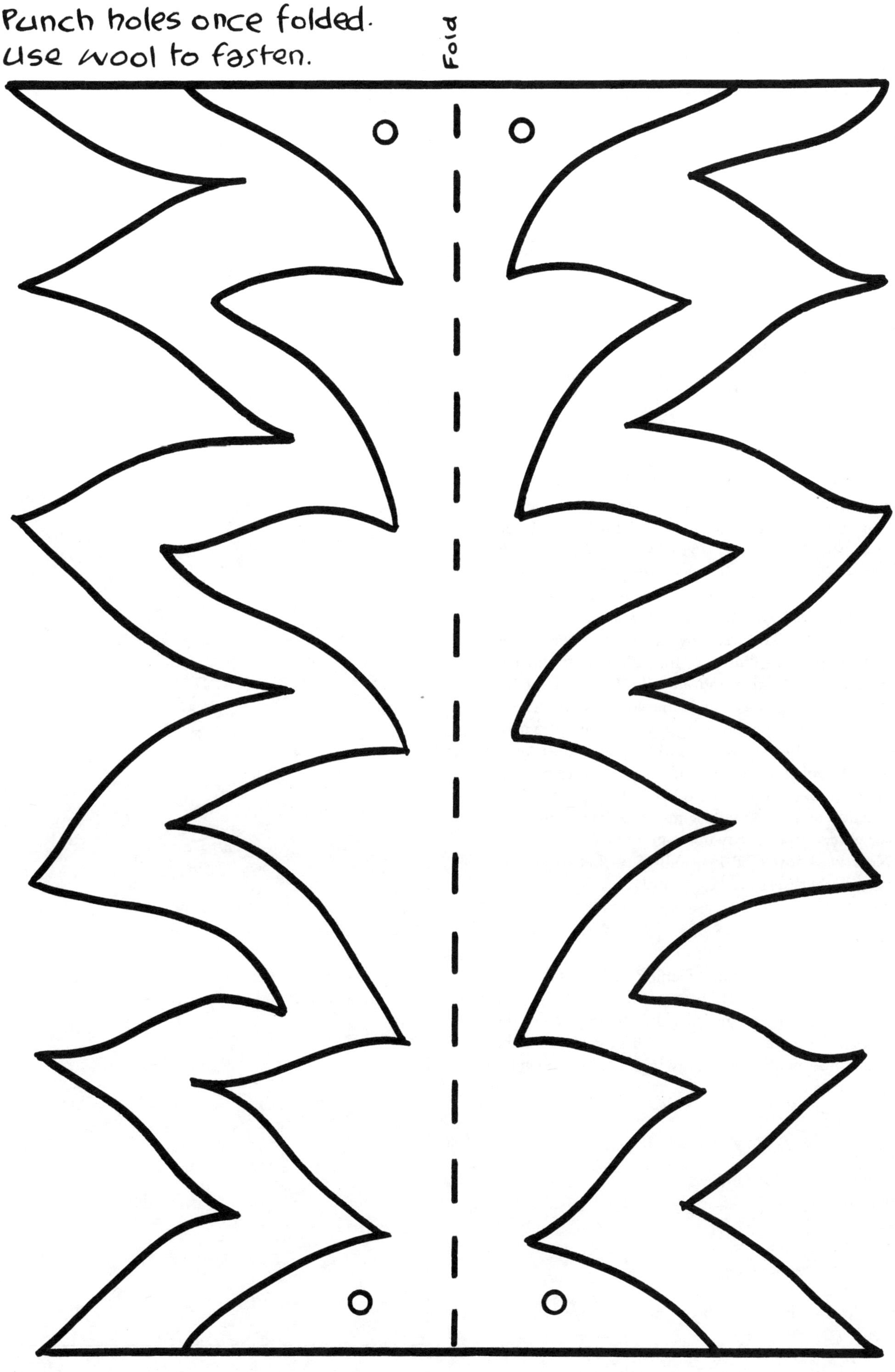

ORDINARY TIME
Trinity Sunday

Aim
To remind the children of their baptism.

Readings
Isaiah 6:1-8
Psalm 29
Romans 8:12-17
John 3:1-17

Teaching
Who knows what happens at the font? Yes, babies and sometimes grown-ups are christened, baptised. Do you know what happens? Let us act it out. We have a bowl of water and a doll. We will have to decide on a name for the doll. (Let the children make suggestions.) What do we do? We put water on the baby's head three times (put three drops on the doll and explain): one for the Father, one for the Son and one for the Holy Spirit. We do this because God made us and loves us. (Repeat with another three drops.) One drop because the Father loves us and wants us to love him, one drop because Jesus loves us and wants us to love him, and one drop because the Holy Spirit loves us and wants us to love him.

Who would like three tiny drops of water on their head to remind us that God, the Father, Son and Holy Spirit, loves us? Go round all volunteers saying their name and saying, 'God the Father loves you' and place a tiny drop of water on their heads. Repeat the action saying, 'Jesus loves you.' A third time go round saying, 'The Holy Spirit loves you.' (If someone does not want to take part, see if they would like to help putting drops on the doll or a friend with some help. Try gently to discover why someone may not want to take part.)

Now we know God loves all of us. Let us sing our song to Father, Son and Holy Spirit.

Activity
To show the children the meaning of baptism, and to help them to know God loves them, make a big poster that says, 'God loves me.' Let the children draw their faces or themselves on the poster. If possible, add their names underneath their drawing. Let the poster be displayed in church.

Prayer
Father God, you love me.
I love you.
Jesus, you love me.
I love you.
Holy Spirit, you love me.
I love you.
Let us love each other always.
Amen.

Song
Father, we adore you

Notes

Draw a picture of yourself in the picture frame and write your name.

Proper 4

Sunday between 29 May and 4 June inclusive
(if after Trinity Sunday)

Aim

To let the children see the love of Jesus.

Readings

1 Samuel 3:1-10 (11-20) or Deuteronomy 5:12-15
Psalm 139:1-6, 13-18 or Psalm 81:1-10
2 Corinthians 4:5-12
Mark 2:23–3:6

Teaching

Once a long time ago there was a man who worked with his hands. He enjoyed making things. He often used a large hammer and chisel. Some days he hit the chisel many times, more than a hundred times. One day a piece of stone broke off the large piece and the man's hand holding the chisel slipped. As it did, he accidentally hit it with the hammer. It caused him a lot of pain. He had to go home and he went to a doctor. His hand could not be made better and it meant he could not use it. His fingers would not work properly. He could not grip the chisel, so he could not do his work. There are lots of things we cannot do if we cannot use two hands.

Who can tie their laces? You cannot do that if you have only one hand. It can be hard to put on your clothes and fasten buttons if you can only use one hand. (Explore the idea of only being able to use one hand.)

The man went to church and often prayed that his hand might get better but it did not. One day Jesus came to the church with his disciples. Jesus wanted to help the man with the injured hand but some of the people said, 'Not today. We do not think God would like you to do it today. Come back another day.' What do you think the man thought? What do you think Jesus thought?

Jesus wanted to make the man better. He wanted to heal him. Jesus said to the man, 'Stretch out your hand.' Everyone could see the hand was hurt and the man could not use it. Jesus hoped they would be sorry for the man and help him, but they would not. Yet while they were all watching, the man's hand got better – it was healed. What do you think this meant for the man? Who do you think made it better? Jesus loved people and wanted them all to be well.

Activity

Let the children draw around their hands and add underneath them, 'Thank you, God, for our hands.'

Play a game of pass the parcel where they must only use their left hand. (This will have to be explained carefully.) The other hand should be kept behind their back. If the parcel is dropped, the person who drops it is out. If two hands are used or the wrong hand, that person is also out. The last person in is the winner and should be given a clap. (Point out that we need two hands to clap.)

Prayer

God, we thank you that you have given us hands.
We clap our hands to thank you:
CLAP, CLAP, CLAP, CLAP.
We clap our hands because we love you:
CLAP, CLAP, CLAP, CLAP.
We clap our hands for Jesus healing the man
with the injured hand:
CLAP, CLAP, CLAP, CLAP.
God, we clap our hands because you are here:
CLAP, CLAP, CLAP, CLAP.

Song

Hands, hands, fingers, thumbs

Notes

Thank you, God, for our hands

Draw round your hand here

For parents and children to pray together

'God, we thank you for our hands. We can draw, we can play, we can use them to eat. Thank you.'

Proper 5

Sunday between 5 and 11 June inclusive (if after Trinity Sunday)

Aim

To show how not everyone loved Jesus.

Readings

1 Samuel 8:4-11 (12-15) 16-20 (11:14-15)
or Genesis 3:8-15
Psalm 138 or Psalm 130
2 Corinthians 4:13–5:1
Mark 3:20-35

Teaching

Jesus was very busy helping people. Wherever he went, large crowds followed him. They wanted to hear him speak, to learn from him. Some wanted to be healed and to be made well by him. (Tell the story of one of the healing miracles to the children, as they need the pictorial images.) Sometimes the crowd was so large Jesus could hardly breathe. When he was by the seaside he sometimes spoke to people from a fishing boat and that stopped the crowds pushing around him. A friend of Jesus told his family at Nazareth that Jesus would wear himself out. He was working too hard and not getting enough rest. Sometimes there was not even time for him to eat.

Mary was worried about her son. She loved him and wanted to protect him. Jesus' brothers came with Mary to the house where he was. They wanted to take him home and look after him, to feed him properly and to care for him. Jesus knew they loved him and cared but he could not go with them. He had to do some special work for God his Father. He wanted everyone to know that God loves them. He wants you to know that God loves you. Even though they loved him, Jesus could not stay at home; he had work to do. (The children can understand this, as parents need to work.)

There were some other people who did not love Jesus. They followed him from Jerusalem to spy on him. They were saying nasty things about him. They knew Jesus was healing people and making them better. But they said Jesus was doing this because he was working with the devil. They tried to say that Jesus was not doing good work. They were against him and his work. This made Jesus very sad because they were telling lies and could not see the goodness.

But Jesus did not stay sad, because he knew that his family loved him and he knew that lots of people were wanting to do what God would like them to do.

Activity

We will draw a picture of our family and say thank you to God for them.

Prayer

We thank you, God, for our homes.
We thank you for food to eat.
We thank you that we can rest.
We thank you for all who love us.
We thank you, that you are with us always.

Song

Jesus' love is very wonderful

Notes

Draw a picture of all your family

For parents and children to pray together

'God, bless our family,
keep them in your love,
keep them safe. Amen.'

Proper 6

Sunday between 12 June and 18 June inclusive
(if after Trinity Sunday)

Aim

To discover how the kingdom of God can grow.

Readings

1 Samuel 15:34–16:13 or Ezekiel 17:22-24
Psalm 20 or Psalm 92:1-4, 12-15
2 Corinthians 5:6-10 (11-13) 14-17
Mark 4:26-34

Teaching

Jonathan Chapman used to travel around farms in America with his Bible. In the evenings he would read to the family; not many of them could read themselves. They looked forward to his visits and they called him 'Johnny Appleseed'.

This is how he got his nickname. On some farms he noticed the men busy making cider. The apples were pressed and when the juice was extracted the pips were thrown away. 'What a waste,' thought Johnny: those little pips could grow into fine trees. So Johnny asked if he could have some seed. The man replied he could have as much seed as he wanted. Johnny filled his saddlebag with seeds. When he visited a farm, in the evening he read from the Bible, then before he left he would make some holes in the soil and plant some apple seeds. He then made a little fence around them to protect them and to give them the chance to grow. For over 40 years Johnny did this work, sowing the word of God in the hearts of people and sowing apple seeds in the ground. Everywhere he went he left something behind to give pleasure and nourishment to the farming people. He understood well that seeds could not grow unless they were planted.

Make a point of showing how all the apple seeds are just thrown away after the cider is made. The seeds are counted as useless. Yet in each seed there is life. In each seed there is an apple tree waiting to be born. If no apple seeds were planted, there would be no apple trees. If you want apple trees, you have to plant seeds. If you want flowers or vegetables in your garden, you have to plant seeds. You will be given a seed or seeds to take home. As long as you look after them, plant them and water them they will grow.

Johnny Appleseed planted seeds in the farms he went to. He also told Bible stories and planted the word of God in the people's hearts. He wanted the people to grow in their love for God. Lots of people grew to know God better and to enjoy the beauty of apple trees because of the work of Johnny Appleseed.

We cannot make things grow. We can plant seeds and water it. But God makes it grow. God has given each seed its own special life. If we do not plant seeds, there will be no new flowers or vegetables. In the same way, if we do not do things for God, his kingdom will not be able to grow in us. God wants us to sow seeds of kindness, of love. He wants to know that we love him as he loves us.

Activity

Let us plant some seeds (give each child a yoghurt carton with a drainage hole in the bottom, seed compost and a runner-bean seed. Get them to fill the cartons with compost. Then make a hole in the compost for their seed. Tell them if they do not put the seed in the hole, it will not grow. Once the seeds are planted, they need to be watered (this could be done at home). We cannot make them grow but we can help them to grow by making sure they are looked after.

Read again Mark 4:26-29 or tell it in your own words. God's kingdom will grow in us if we try to be kind and loving, if we seek to be good and generous.

Make a date in about three weeks' time for them to bring any growing seeds.

Prayer

God, we thank you for seeds,
for the seeds of flowers, fruit and vegetables.
We thank you for seeds of trees and bushes and grasses,
for seeds that make bread and for rice seeds.
May we grow in our love for you
and be part of your kingdom.
Amen.

Song

There are hundreds of sparrows

Notes

Colour then cut out

—

Fold one section under another then unfold to make the tree grow.

—

Proper 7

Sunday between 19 and 25 June inclusive (if after Trinity Sunday)

Aim

To show how Jesus keeps us safe.

Readings

1 Samuel 17:(1a, 4-11, 19-23) 32-49
or 1 Samuel 17:57–18:5, 10-16 or Job 38:1-11
Psalm 9:9-20 or Psalm 133 or Psalm 107:1-3, 23-32
2 Corinthians 6:1-13
Mark 4:35-41

Teaching

Begin by talking how the children feel safe when they have a parent or someone to look after them. Discover how they are not afraid of the dark if someone who loves them is near.

One evening Jesus was very tired. He had been working very hard and needed to rest. The disciples who were fishermen took him into their boat away from the crowds. Soon Jesus was asleep on a seat in the back of the boat. The disciples raised the sail and pulled on the oars and soon they were right out at sea. (Get the children to pretend to raise the sails and to row.) They were now out in the middle of the sea and the water was very deep. Jesus was fast asleep.

Suddenly the wind started to blow. Let us make the sound of the wind. It was much louder than that – let us make the sound bigger! The wind rushed down the hills and blew on to the sea. The waves rose up and they slapped into the boat (clap your hands as you say this). The wind got louder and the waves grew higher. Let us make the sounds of the wind and the waves. The disciples were frightened their boat was going to sink.

If they did not get some of the water out of the boat, the boat would sink and they would all be in the sea. They took the sail down and rowed hard (actions). They tried to get some of the water out of the boat (actions). The wind kept blowing and the waves got bigger (actions).

All this time Jesus was asleep in the back of the boat. He trusted in God his Father and was able to sleep even in the storm. The disciples needed his help. The boat was rocking from side to side (action). The disciples were frightened and they woke Jesus up, shouting, 'Teacher, save us.' Let us shout those words again.

Jesus awoke to the sound of the wind and the waves and the boat rocking (actions). He stood up and said in a loud voice, 'Peace! Be still!' The wind and the waves obeyed him. The wind stopped blowing and the sea became calm. All was quiet. The disciples were amazed: only one person could make the wind stop and the waves to be still and that was God. So who must Jesus be? Jesus is God. The disciples were very happy because they were not afraid any more. They felt safe to be with Jesus.

Activity

If possible, have a little boat and a large bowl for it to sail in. Let the children make the water stormy and put little bits of water in the boat. Rescue the boat before it sinks. On the worksheet there is a boat and a stormy sea to be coloured.

Prayer

Jesus, we thank you that you stilled the storm
and saved the disciples.
You are with us always.
Help us when we are afraid.
Amen.

Song

Wide, wide as the ocean

Notes

For parents and children to pray together

'Lord Jesus, when
it is dark or stormy,
help us to know
you are with us.
You are strong
and love us.
Amen.'

Proper 8

Sunday between 26 June and 2 July inclusive

Aim

To show that by touching the girl Jesus gave her life back to her.

Readings

2 Samuel 1:1, 17-27 or
Wisdom of Solomon 1:13-15; 2:23-24
Psalm 130 or Psalm 30 or Lamentations 3:23-33.
2 Corinthians 8:7-15
Mark 5:21-43

Teaching

Begin by welcoming back to the class anyone who has been ill. When (Sam) was poorly his mother and father were really sad. They wanted him to be well and happy. Now that he is well again they are very happy. Today's story is about a little girl who was very ill and it made her mother and father very sad. This is also a story about Jesus and the girl's father Jairus. (Let us say his name together.)

Jairus lived in a lovely white house with his wife and daughter. He was an important man and looked after the church. One day when he came home he noticed the house was very quiet – there was no little girl running about. Mummy came and said their girl was in bed because she was not very well. Jairus got the doctor to call but he said she could not be made well. Mummy and Daddy sat by her bedside. They held her hands but the little girl did not open her eyes. She was very poorly and they did not know what to do.

Suddenly Jairus turned to his wife and said, 'I know what to do. Remember there is someone who has been healing people and making them well again. Do you remember he cured the man with the withered hand? (Explain.) Well, I am going to find him and bring him to our home and to our daughter. 'Good,' said Mummy, 'go as quickly as you can because she is very poorly.'

Jairus ran as fast as he could. He pushed through the crowds to where Jesus was and knelt down at his feet. Everyone was amazed to see the man who looked after their church kneeling before Jesus. 'Oh Jesus, come to my house and heal my little girl or she will die.' Everyone heard and they were so sad for the man. They wondered what Jesus would do. Jesus said he would go now and they set off for the house. Then a very sad man came running and said, 'Don't bother to bring Jesus: your little girl has died.' Jairus began to cry because his little girl was dead. Jesus said to him, 'I will still come with you. Do not be afraid; only believe.' When they got to the house people were playing sad music, others were crying loudly – it was all very sad. They told Jesus he was too late to do anything. Jesus asked them all to go outside the house. He went in with the girl's mummy and daddy and three of his disciples. They all went into the bedroom and saw the little girl lying very still upon the bed with her eyes closed. Jesus went over, took hold of her cold hands and said to her, 'Get up, my little girl.' He could feel her hands get warm. She opened her eyes and smiled at Jesus. Then she got up out of bed and stood up on her own two feet. Jesus told them to give her some food to make her strong again. How happy her mummy and daddy were, because Jesus had come to their house and by touching the girl had made her well again.

Activity

Play a game of tag. Once a person is touched they join the person who started and go around touching others. The last person to be touched becomes the new leader. All who were touched have to sit or lie on the ground until the new leader goes around and touches them and gives them 'new life'. If time allows, play this three or four times.

Prayer

Lord Jesus, we thank you for our lives
and that you love us.
We thank you that you healed the little girl
and we ask that you will look after us.
Amen.

Song

Jesus, friend of little children

Notes

For parents and children to pray together:

'Jesus, we thank you for rest and pray that you look after us.'

Proper 9

Sunday between 3 and 9 July inclusive

Aim

To show that Jesus wants us to listen and to talk about him to others.

Readings

2 Samuel 5:1-5, 9-10 or Ezekiel 2:1-5
Psalm 48 or Psalm 123
2 Corinthians 12:2-10
Mark 6:1-13

Teaching

Who knows how many disciples Jesus had? It was twelve. (Let us count to twelve.) They were his special friends who went with him and listened to all that he told them. They listened carefully to him. (Let us be very quiet and listen. Do you hear any sounds?) We will play a listening game. (Choose someone to make the sound of an animal and the rest have to guess what it is. The one who gets it right can make the next sound.)

Naughty Nigel never listened. When someone was talking to him he often talked as well. He did not want to hear when he was told to go and do something so he kept his ears shut. At school he did not learn because he would not listen. When his mummy spoke to him he did not hear because he was listening to the television. When his daddy asked him to do something he did not hear because he was thinking about his toys. Naughty Nigel would not listen. He was told not to go into an old building because it was dangerous. Nigel would not listen and went in with another naughty boy. They climbed some old stairs but when they got near the top, the stairs all fell down and so did Nigel and his friend. Nigel had to go to hospital with a broken leg. He knew this had happened because he would not listen. From now on he promised to listen carefully.

Jesus wanted his twelve disciples to go and tell other people about him. He chose the twelve because they listened to him and went around with him. They knew him best of all. He sent them out to villages and towns to tell people the Good News of God's love and to heal people and make them well again. He sent them out in twos so that they could help each other and be friends with each other. If there were twelve and they were sent out in twos, how many twos were there? (Get twelve children to come out and divide them into twos to show it was six twos. Let the children count the twelve and the six.)

Wherever the disciples went people welcomed them because they had Good News to tell them. The disciples showed the people the power of Jesus by healing and helping them. But there were some people who would not listen. Some people said they were too busy. Some could not be bothered. Others talked too much to hear anyone else but themselves. So some people missed the Good News and some people missed being made well again. It was rather sad that they would not listen. When the disciples came back and told Jesus, he was sorry that some would not listen. But some did not listen even to him.

Now I will see who has been listening. I will ask you some questions. (Review today's lesson, which is quite hard for little ones.) Jesus likes people who are able to listen carefully and then tell others about him. Tell me what you know about Jesus.

Activity

We will play 'Sleepy tigers'. One person must sit out in front and count to ten. She watches whilst the others lie down and go to sleep. The tigers must not move at all. Anyone who is seen moving must sit out with the person at the front and watch for twitching tigers. The last person is the King of the Jungle and becomes the next one to count.

Prayer

Jesus, we love you and like being quiet with you.
We like the stories about you
and that you want us to be your disciples.
Amen.

Song

I'm singing your praise, Lord

Notes

Count the disciples.
How many twos?
How many going to tell others about Jesus?

Colour the picture.

For parents and children to pray together:

'Thank you, God, for all who have told us about you, and thank you for Jesus.'

Proper 10

Sunday between 10 and 16 July inclusive

Aim

To show the wickedness of Herod and the goodness of God's kingdom.

Readings

2 Samuel 6:1-5, 12b-19 or Amos 7:7-15
Psalm 24 or Psalm 85:8-13
Ephesians 1:3-14
Mark 6:14-29

Teaching

Once there was a wicked king who lived in a big castle beside the Dead Sea. If he did not like what you said, he sent his soldiers to capture and put you in his prison. His prison was underneath the castle and it was dark and cold and damp. This king was called Herod. John the Baptist, who was a cousin of Jesus, said King Herod should not be so wicked. He should turn away from wickedness and do good. This just made the king angry. He sent his soldiers and took John a prisoner. He had him put in the dungeons of his castle.

The wicked King Herod had a birthday and he asked all sorts of people to his party. He asked people from his palace, and he asked important people, rich people. He asked those who would help him and give him things. At the party his daughter Salome came and danced for them. The king was very pleased with her dancing and offered her a present – anything she wanted. What do you think you would choose? She could have silver or jewels or gold, even part of the king's kingdom. She thought for a moment or two and then asked her mother what she should ask for. Her mother, Herodias, did not like John the Baptist and she asked for a terrible thing. She asked for the head of John the Baptist on a plate. Even though the king was wicked he did not want to do this. I think he was a little frightened of John the Baptist. But he promised. So he sent his soldiers down into the prison to where John was and had John's head cut off and put on a plate. It was a terrible thing to do but it pleased the wicked queen. John's friends came and took his body away and buried it.

Not far away was another King, though most people did not know he was a king. He did not have a castle and he did not wear rich clothes. He did not have soldiers to protect him. He only had twelve friends who went with him and helped him. He also had a party. It was not his birthday but he saw that the people were hungry and tired and he wanted to help them. He did not check to see if they were rich or poor. He loved them and got his friends, the disciples, to feed them. Who knows the name of this kind king?

Jesus wants us all to be happy and to be free to do what is good and kind in this world. He wants to help us as much as he can.

Which king would you like to look after you: the wicked King Herod or Jesus the King of love? (Let the children explore this for a while.)

Activity

Have five cards with a large club on one side and a large heart on the other side. The corners of the room will each have a person with a card and there will be someone in the centre of the room with a card. The children run around the room to music. When the music stops they must run to a corner. The people with cards in the corners will produce them and show a black club or a red heart. Black clubs are for the wicked king and all these children are out. If all cards are black, the person in the centre shows a red heart and all are set free to run again. The corners with the red hearts are corners for the King of love: when the music starts the children in red corners can join the game again.

Prayer

Jesus, you are the King of love.
We thank you for being so kind and gentle.
Help us to be kind and gentle too.
Amen.

Song

We're the kids of the King

Notes

Colour a crown for Jesus

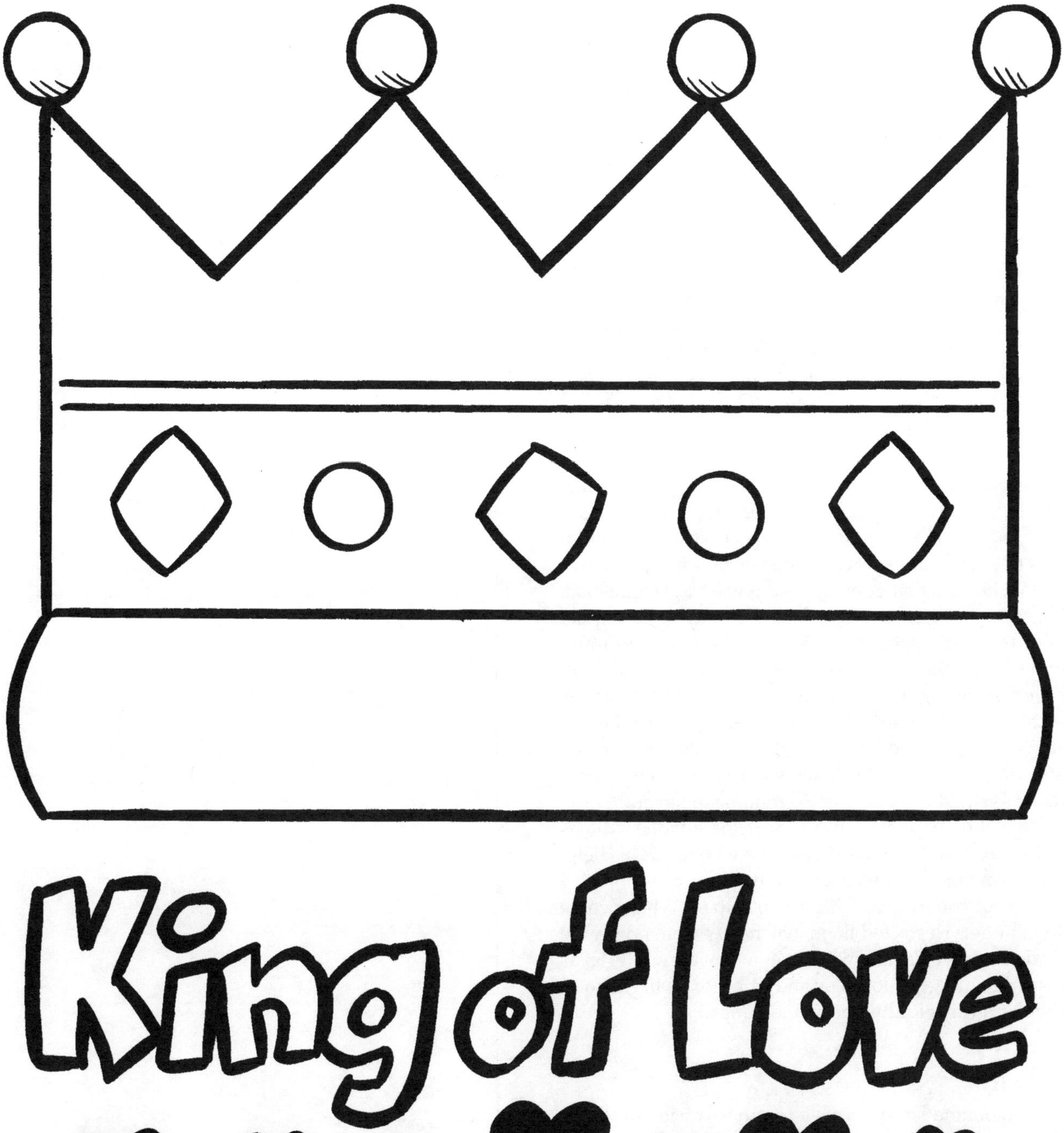

King of Love

For parents and children to pray together

'Jesus, you are our King and our God. We love you.'

Proper 11

Sunday between 17 and 23 July inclusive

Aim
To show that Jesus loves each one of us and wants us to love him.

Readings
2 Samuel 7:1-14a or Jeremiah 23:1-6
Psalm 89:20-37 or Psalm 23
Ephesians 2:11-22
Mark 6:30-34, 53-56

Teaching
Do you know the story of the lost lamb? It was an adventurous little lamb which wanted to see what was around the next corner or over the top of the next hill. It walked and walked and walked, until it was tired. Then it lay down to sleep. When it woke it was still dark and it did not know where it was. It started to cry, 'Maa, maa, maa.' (Let us make that sound.) It was calling for its mother but its mother could not hear it. Again it cried, 'Maa, maa, maa.' (Let us make the sound again.) As it was getting light, the little lamb was very hungry and it was not very happy. It would never find its way home. Then it heard a lion growling and it was very frightened. It knew that lions eat little lambs. It stayed very quiet until the lion went away. Poor little lamb was lost and hungry. But the shepherd was a good man and he had been out all night looking for it. He shouted its name, 'Aggy.' For a long time he heard nothing; then, when he shouted 'Aggy', he heard a little cry. 'Maa, maa, maa.' He hurried to where the lamb was and picked it up, put it on his shoulders and carried it home to its mother.

Like the shepherd, Jesus cares for anyone who is hungry or lost. He looks for anyone who needs his help. Jesus wants to help us if we are frightened or not very well. Jesus comes to be with and to help us. When people were hungry, Jesus fed them; when they were poorly, he made them well again; when they were in trouble, Jesus helped them. Jesus loves us and cares for us like a good shepherd cares for his sheep and lambs.

Activity
Play 'Lion and sheep'. This is another version of 'What time is it, Mr Wolf?'

The children follow behind the one chosen to be the Lion, saying, 'Baa, baa, baa, what are you doing?' The Lion replies, 'I am walking in the desert' and keeps on walking. When the Lion says, 'I am hungry', he chases the sheep and the one he catches or the last one back to the safety of base becomes the next lion.

Prayer
Jesus, thank you for loving us.
We know that you are the Good Shepherd
and that you care for us and come to us.
We give our love to you.
Amen.

Song
Jesus is our shepherd

Notes

The Lost Sheep.
Cut it out and put it in the shepherd's arms.

A sheep is lost

A sheep is found

For parents and children to pray together

'Jesus, you are the Good Shepherd. You care for us and seek us when we feel lost. Thank you. Amen.'

Proper 12

Sunday between 24 and 30 July inclusive

Aim

To show how Jesus cares for people and seeks help even from children.

Readings

2 Samuel 11:1-15 or 2 Kings 4:42-44
Psalm 14 or Psalm 145:10-18
Ephesians 3:14-21
John 6:1-21

Teaching

Have you ever gone for a long walk in the country? What did you do for food? It is nice to take a picnic. (Talk a little about picnics.)

Once there were a lot of people walking around the edge of the sea. They wanted to go to where Jesus was and they were walking for about half a day. Most of them had set off suddenly and did not take any food with them, though there was one little lad who had a picnic. He had five little loaves – they were really rolls – and two tiny fish. (Bring out a basket at this point with five little loaves in it and two small fish, all made from playdough or plasticine). Look, this is what his mummy gave him. (Let them count the loaves and fishes and then put them away again until Andrew brings the basket to Jesus.)

More and more people gathered on a grassy hillside to listen to Jesus or to be healed by him. They were there until late in the afternoon and by now they were hungry. The disciples thought that Jesus should tell them to go home because it was getting late and they all looked hungry. Jesus knew what he was going to do but he asked Philip, 'Where can we get bread for these people to eat?' Philip said, 'There is nowhere to buy food and even if there was I would have to work for half a year just to be able to pay for them to have a little.'

Andrew noticed the little boy with the basket and told Jesus, 'There is a little lad with five loaves and two small fish.' Jesus asked if he could have the food and the boy said he could. 'But,' said Andrew, 'it is such a small amount, and there must be about 5000 people. You would have to share a loaf amongst 1000 people.'

Jesus smiled and told the disciples to ask the people to sit down. Then he took the loaves and fishes into his hands. He looked up to heaven and thanked God for this food the boy had given. He then began to break it and share it. He gave it to the disciples and the disciples gave it to the people. A wonderful thing happened. As Jesus gave the disciples the bread, it did not run out – there was enough for everyone there. He did the same with the fish. There was even a lot left at the end.

The little boy was so pleased that he had given Jesus his picnic. When he got home he would tell his mother how his picnic of five loaves and two fish had fed 5000 people.

In the large crowd Jesus and his friends had noticed one little boy and asked him to help them. Because one child was willing to help Jesus, Jesus was able to feed 5000 people.

Activity

Let each child make the loaves and fishes with playdough or plasticine. They can also colour the five loaves and the two fish on their worksheet.

Help the children to understand the song. Read it to them. Sing a verse and then get them to sing a verse.

Prayer

Jesus, thank you for letting the little boy help you.
We would like to help you
and do what you want us to do.
Amen.

Song

5 0 0 0 + hungry folk

Notes

Andrew
Jesus with bread
Boy
How many loaves?
How many fish?
For parents and children to pray together.
'Thank you, God,
for the food
we eat. Amen.'

Proper 13

Sunday between 31 July and 6 August inclusive

Aim

To show how God fed his people when they were hungry.

Readings

2 Samuel 11:26–12:13a or Exodus 16:2-4, 9-15
Psalm 51:1-12 or Psalm 78:23-29
Ephesians 4:1-6
John 6:24-35

Teaching

Have you ever walked a long way in the countryside? Did you take a picnic or did you go and get some food somewhere? Once the people who escaped from the wicked king in Egypt walked a long way through the desert. They walked for days and for years. They had to walk and walk and walk. After a while all the food that they had brought with them had gone; they had eaten it. Some children began to cry because they were very hungry. But their mothers and fathers had no food to give them and they were hungry too. 'I wish we had stayed with the wicked king; at least we had food.' They went and grumbled to their leader Moses and blamed him for their being hungry.

Moses was very sad because he could not help them. But he was even sadder because they forgot that God was looking after them. 'Do you not remember that God helped you to escape from the wicked king? God has kept you safe and helped you to cross the sea. God has always cared for you – don't you think he will help you now?'

Moses went away to a quiet place by himself and said his prayers to God. God then told Moses, 'Do not worry. I will look after the people.' Then he told Moses what he was going to do.

Moses got all the people together and said, 'God is going to give you bread from heaven each day. You must go out every day and collect it. Do not be greedy; just collect enough for everyone in your family.'

The next morning there was something white scattered all over the ground. Everybody asked, 'Manna?' (which means 'What is it?'). They picked it up and said, 'Manna.' (Let us say it: 'Manna.') They turned it over and looked at it, and smelt it and asked, 'Manna? What is it?' Then someone tasted it and it tasted sweet and lovely. 'It tastes lovely, we can eat it.' Soon everyone was excited and they were collecting manna until there was a bowlful for each person. Some of the children would have gone on collecting but they were told only to collect enough for the day. God would give them some more the next day.

Everyone ate the manna. How nice it tasted! No one was hungry any more. God had sent the people food when they needed it. The next day there was more and they still called it manna. They scooped it up into bowls and collected it for their food. They all said thank you to God for giving them food and for loving them.

Activity

Have teams of about six children. Scatter a cupful of rice or confetti on large sheets of brown paper. Tell the children they are to pick it all up piece by piece and each time they have a few pieces to put them in the cup and, as they put it in, say, 'Manna'. It is not a race but we would like to see all the cups full again and nothing left lying about.

Prayer

God, thank you for loving us,
for giving us food to eat.
We know that you care for us
and for everything that you have made. Amen.

Song

There are hundreds of sparrows

Notes

Manna?

What is it?

For parents and children to pray together.

'Thank you for the world so sweet,
Thank you for the food we eat,
Thank you for the birds that sing,
Thank you, God, for everything.'

Edith Rutter Leatham

Proper 14

Sunday between 7 and 13 August inclusive

Aim

To show how God cares for Elijah, and to suggest he cares for us in the same way.

Readings

2 Samuel 18:5-9, 31-33 or 1 Kings 19:4-8
Psalm 130 or Psalm 34:1-8
Ephesians 4:25–5:2
John 6:35, 41-51

Teaching

Today we are going to learn about someone who worked very hard for God. He was called Elijah. (Would you like to say his name after me? Elijah. Would anyone like to say it by himself or herself?) Elijah was a strong man and not afraid to tell people about God. He showed the people how God loved them and cared for them. Elijah did wonderful works for God. He was a good and brave man.

But there was a wicked queen who did not like Elijah. She was called Jezebel (Would you like to say her name?) The wicked queen had an army and she wanted to capture Elijah and kill him. Poor Elijah felt so tired and now he was afraid. He would have to hide from Queen Jezebel. He went away into a wild place where no one lived. It was a desert place (see if the children know what a desert is); nothing much grew there and there was no food. There was a single tree – just one all by itself. Elijah tried to get some shelter from the sun under the shade of the tree. He was so tired and hungry. There was no food and he was sure he would die. He lay under the tree and went to sleep.

Suddenly there was someone shaking him and making him wake up. He opened his eyes and saw a messenger from God, one of God's angels. The angel touched him and said, 'Get up and eat, or the journey will be too hard for you.' Elijah rubbed his eyes in case he was dreaming. But there was the angel and there was a loaf baked on hot stones and there was a jar of water. Elijah got up and ate and drank. He knew that God cared for him and loved him. He then lay down again and had a good sleep. The angel of God came a second time and woke him again. There was a nice smell of wood smoke and baking. Again there was food for Elijah to eat. This would make him strong and able to go across the desert. Elijah felt so much better. God had sent him food and new strength. He would now be able to go to God's mountain and escape from the wicked queen.

Activity

Play the game 'Elijah and Jezebel'. Let two children be blindfolded; one is Elijah and the other is Jezebel. The aim is for Jezebel to catch Elijah. Jezebel calls out, 'Elijah!' and he has to reply 'Jezebel!' Jezebel keeps shouting to get a reply and guess where he is. Elijah keeps on the move. If Jezebel manages to capture Elijah, an 'angel' removes his blindfold and helps him escape before Jezebel's blindfold is removed.

Prayer

God our Father, we thank you for caring for us
and providing us with food.
We know that you love us
and this makes us happy.
Amen.

Song

Praise him, praise him

Notes

Follow the path to bring food to tired Elijah

For parents and children to pray together.

'God, thank you for food.
Thank you for love.
Thank you for angels.'

Proper 15

Sunday between 14 and 20 August inclusive

Aim

To introduce the idea of the bread and wine as a remembrance of Jesus.

Readings

1 Kings 2:10-12; 3:3-14 or Proverbs 9:1-6
Psalm 111 or Psalm 34:9-14
Ephesians 5:15-20
John 6:51-58

Teaching

How do we remember our relatives and friends? We have photographs and presents that they gave us. Have you got photographs at home of your grandmother or grandfather? You may have a photograph of a brother or sister who has left home. Sometimes we have photographs or pictures of places we have been to remind us how nice they are. Here are some of my photographs of my family and some of the places I like. (Show photographs – if you prefer you can show photographs of famous people from magazines and see if the children recognise them.)

In the time of Jesus there were no photographs or magazines. If you wanted someone to remember you, you had to give him or her something that would make them think of you. Jesus decided to give his disciples two things to remind them always of him. (If possible, show a chalice and a paten and see if the children recognise what they are for – a photograph could suffice.) Jesus did not give silver or gold; he gave the disciples bread and wine. He wanted them to remember him through bread and wine. To remember he fed 5000 people. Do you remember? To remember he took bread, broke it and gave it to them. He said he would be with them when they broke bread. (Explain how they did not cut bread but broke it. Take a piece of bread, break it and give it to the children and say, 'Remember Jesus'.)

Jesus also gave the disciples wine. 'Remember how I turned water into wine at the wedding.'

The disciples met often to break bread together and to drink the wine and to remember Jesus. The wine was red and it reminded them how Jesus died on the cross and gave his life for them. They remembered that Jesus was with them even though they could not see him. Every time they took bread and wine they gave thanks for Jesus: that he gave his life for them and that he rose again.

Activity

Have a pack of cards – you can buy packs with nice pictures on them – and turn them all face downwards. The children have to pick two that are the same. If they fail, they show the two cards and put them back carefully. If there are less than 26 children in the class, make sure there are only enough cards for two each.

Prayer

Jesus, help us to remember you each day
and to give our love to you.
Amen.

Song

Jesus' love is very wonderful

Notes

Remember me

For parents and children to pray together:

Jesus, help us to remember you and your love through the bread and wine.

Proper 16

Sunday between 21 and 27 August inclusive

Aim

To know that God loves us and protects us.

Readings

1 Kings 8:(1, 6, 10-11) 22-30, 41-43 or Joshua 24:1-2a, 14-18
Psalm 84 or Psalm 34:15-22
Ephesians 6:10-20
John 6:56-69

Teaching

If you are going out and it starts to rain, what do you put on? Waterproofs, a raincoat, wellingtons, and you might have an umbrella.

If it is very hot and sunny, what do you use to protect yourself? You might wear sunglasses, sun cream; you might have a parasol. What is the difference between an umbrella and a parasol? (If possible, show these to the children.)

Now, if it is very cold, what do you wear? Gloves, scarf, coat, snow boots: you wrap up to keep warm.

If you are riding a bike or on a skateboard, what sort of things do you wear? You need a helmet, some knee pads and some elbow pads to protect you in case you fall off.

Let us pretend we are getting ready to go out. It is raining: let us put on our rainwear and put up an umbrella.

Now it's hot and sunny: let us take off our rainwear and put on our sunglasses and put up a sunshade.

Now it is suddenly becoming cold: we put away the sunshade and get out our gloves and scarves and put on a big coat.

Show some toy armour or a picture of a Roman soldier in armour. Now, what do you think this is for? It is to protect the soldier from the enemy, to save him from getting hurt. His helmet is to stop his head getting hurt. His shield and breastplate are to stop arrows or someone with a sword from hitting him. The Roman soldier feels stronger and safer in his armour. (Let one of the children put on the toy armour if you have some.)

God knows that sometimes the world is a dangerous place and he wants to protect us. He comes to us to give us his strength. If we know he is there, it makes us strong. If it is dark and we have a light, it makes us braver and happier. When we know that God loves us and protects us, it also makes us braver and happier. God is always with us, and when we are in trouble, he especially wants to care for us and keep us from harm.

Activity

Play 'Musical hats'. Have two or three funny hats. The children stand in a circle all facing in one direction so that they look at the back of each other's heads. During the music a hat is placed on their heads from behind. They then take the hat off and place it on the head in front. Those caught with a hat on their head when the music stops are out. So it continues until the circle is small and only one is left.

Prayer

O God, thank you for your love.
We are happy that you care for us
and protect us from all evil.
Amen.

Song

We are marching in the light of God

(Have the second verse – 'We are marching in the strength of God'. Let the children march around as they sing this. The music could be used for 'Musical hats' so that the children become familiar with it.)

Notes

For parents and children to pray together.

'God, thank you for protecting us and keeping us safe by your strength.'

Proper 17

Sunday between 28 August and 3 September inclusive

Aim

To show God wants all of us, not just our prayers.

Readings

Song of Solomon 2:8-13 or Deuteronomy 4:1-2, 6-9
Psalm 45:1-2, 6-9 or Psalm 15
James 1:17-27
Mark 7:1-8, 14-15, 21-23

Teaching

Who gets your breakfast ready? Who washes your clothes? Who sees that you are happy and loved? You are lucky that someone loves you and gives themselves to you. Your mother and father show their love by what they give you, but more important they give you of themselves. They give you their time, their attention and their love. It is good to know that you are not left alone. When you go home you can depend on someone being there.

Jesus likes us to speak to him in prayer. Jesus likes us to come to church. Jesus likes us to try and be good, but most of all he likes us to give ourselves to him – not just our prayers or our songs but our whole self in love. We will learn a new song that tells us this:

Jesus wants all of me,
Jesus wants all of me,
Jesus wants all of me,
that's what he wants.
(*Repeat*)

My heart, my mind, my hands, my feet, my ears, my nose, my eyes, my teeth, my arms, my legs, my toes, my knees.

Get the children to repeat the first verse a few times before they sing it.

Go through the second verse getting them to point at each part of the body. Let them wave their hands, jump with their feet, swing their arms, shake their legs, wiggle their toes and knock their knees together. Go through the actions a few times before they attempt it to music.

End with shouting, 'What does Jesus want?' and let them reply loudly, 'Jesus wants all of me'.

Activity

Play 'Simon says'. Choose someone to stand out in front. They are to tell the others what to do. You must obey when he/she starts with 'Simon says' But if he/she omits starting with 'Simon says', you must stand absolutely still. If you move the least bit you are out. The last person in is the next Simon/Simone.

Prayer

God, we love you.
You have made us and you love us.
We want to give ourselves to you.
Amen.

Song

Jesus wants all of me

Notes

Cross out every word with a star *

What does Jesus Want?

For parents and children to pray together

'God, thank you for the world. We love you and give you our lives, our home, our family. Keep us safe in your love.'

Proper 18

Sunday between 4 and 10 September inclusive

Aim

To help the children understand the wonderful healing of the man suffering from deafness.

Readings

Proverbs 22:1-2, 8-9, 22-23 or Isaiah 35:4-7a
Psalm 125 or Psalm 146
James 2:1-10 (11-13) 14-17
Mark 7:24-37

Teaching

There are many people in the world who cannot hear. Do you know what you call it when you cannot hear? Anyone who cannot hear is said to be 'deaf'. Say it after me: 'deaf'. If you suffer from deafness you cannot hear anything. You cannot hear the birds singing. You cannot hear someone speaking. What else would you not hear? Let us pretend we are not able to hear. Cover your ears with the flat of your hands. (Once this is done, mouth words to the children but do not say them.) Mime that they should take their hands off their ears.

If you do not hear words, you cannot learn them. So many people who suffer from deafness cannot speak properly either. They have never heard words so they do not know how to say them. They have to learn to talk through actions. If they want something, they can point or show it by actions. Try a few simple mimes and see if the children can understand. Mime 'I am hungry', 'I am tired', 'I will go upstairs', 'I love you'. Do not worry if the children do not get all the answers. Shake your head when they are wrong and nod when they are right. Help them to see how difficult it is.

Now we will use our ears and listen to a story. There was once a man who could not hear: he was deaf. So he could not hear about Jesus and how wonderful Jesus is. The man could not speak properly because he had not heard words. So he could not ask to be taken to Jesus. The man had some friends who cared for him and wished that he could get better. When the friends heard that Jesus was near where they lived they got very excited. Maybe Jesus could make their friend better. By signs they invited their friend to go out for a walk. (Indicate this by walking fingers.) They brought him to Jesus.

Jesus could see that the man was unable to hear so he took him away from the crowd. He led him by the hand. Then Jesus acted out what he wanted to do. He put his fingers gently into the man's ears. Then he touched the man's tongue. Looking closely at the man, Jesus said, 'Be opened.' Jesus was speaking to the man's ears and to his mouth. And the man heard him. This was the first time the man had heard anything. Jesus made the man able to hear and to speak.

Everyone was very excited and they said about Jesus, 'He has done everything well; he makes the deaf to hear and the dumb to speak.'

Activity

Show drawings of various things and ask what noise they make – for example, a cat, dog, alarm clock, bell, aeroplane, bird. Let the children make the noise of something for others to guess what it is. They may also like to react to sign language. Use your hands to welcome them – open arms and smiley face. Turn them away with pushing-out action of arms. Beckon them back with a wave of the hand. You could make this into a little game.

Prayer

God, we thank you for ears to hear
and a mouth to speak.
May we listen carefully to what we are told
and enjoy singing songs about you.
Amen.

Song

Lord, you put a tongue in my mouth

Notes

Make the sounds of

For parents and children to pray together

'God, thank you for our ears and all the sounds we hear. We pray for all who are deaf.'

Proper 19

Sunday between 11 and 17 September inclusive

Aim

To review what the children know about Jesus.

Readings

Proverbs 1:20-33 or Isaiah 50:4-9a
Psalm 19 or Wisdom of Solomon 7:26–8:1 or Psalm 116:1-9
James 3:1-12
Mark 8:27-38

Teaching

Lots of names have meanings. Perhaps even yours.

Peter = Rock or Rocky
John = Jonah = Dove   means God is Gracious
Abigail = Servant
Christopher = one who carries Christ

(Encourage the children to talk about names and meanings.)

Jesus = Saviour; the one who rescues people.

Who can tell me where Jesus was born? Yes, it was in Bethlehem, in a stable. Can you remember who his mother was? She was called Mary.

When Jesus was born there were shepherds on the hillsides and they heard angels singing, 'Glory to God in the highest.' The angels also said, 'To you is born in the city of David a Saviour, who is Christ, the Lord.'

What do you call the day when Jesus was born? Christmas Day. It has one of the names of Jesus in it. Who knows what it is?

Christ means that Jesus was God's special chosen one. It reminds us that God sent his Son Jesus to help us when we are in trouble.

Once when the friends of Jesus were sitting by a campfire Jesus asked if they knew who he really was. Peter said, 'You are the Christ.' He knew that Jesus was God's chosen one. God had especially sent Jesus to show us all about his love. (You could encourage the children to talk about some of the wonderful things Jesus did.)

Who knows how Jesus died? It was on Good Friday. He died on a cross. (Show a picture or crucifix and let the children talk about it.) After he died he was buried in a cave in a hillside. But that was not the end for Jesus Christ. What happened next? He was alive again and was seen by his disciples. Who knows what you call the day when Jesus awoke from the dead? It is Easter Day and we are all happy on Easter Day because Jesus Christ is alive.

We cannot see Jesus but we know he loves us and is with us always. How do we speak to Jesus? Through our prayers we speak to Jesus.

Activity

Play 'Stuck in the mud'. Whenever a person is tagged they have to stand with legs apart and arms outstretched. A player who has not been tagged can crawl through their legs and set them free again. You may need more than one 'It' to tag people or people will be freed too easily.

Prayer

Jesus, we are happy that you love us
and want us to be your friends.
We come in the quiet to be with you.
Amen.

Song

Wide, wide as the ocean

Notes

Bethlehem

Christmas

You are the Christ

Good Friday

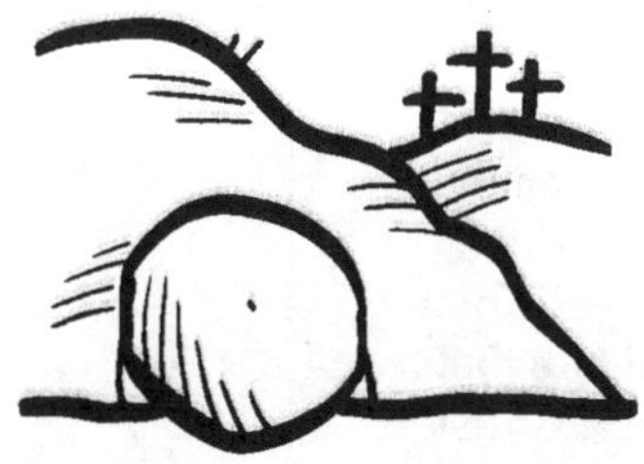

Christ buried

Christ is alive

Colour the candle

CHRIST IS RISEN

For parents and children to pray together

'Jesus Christ, we are happy that you are alive and you want to be our friend.'

Proper 20

Sunday between 18 and 24 September inclusive

Aim

To show that by caring for others we find Jesus comes to us.

Readings

Proverbs 31:10-31 or Wisdom of Solomon 1:16–2:1, 12-22 or Jeremiah 11:18-20
Psalm 1 or Psalm 54
James 3:13–4:3, 7-8a
Mark 9:30-37

Teaching

There was once a strong young man called Offero. He lived in a mountain area where there were great waterfalls and deep streams. Because he was strong he decided he would like to work for the strongest person of all. When he enquired, he was told about many strong people but then he was told the devil was even stronger than them all. He wondered if he should serve the devil. Then he saw someone making the sign of the cross and was told that they did it because Jesus Christ was stronger than the devil; that Jesus' love was stronger than wickedness. Offero decided he would like to work for Jesus Christ but did not know how to do it. A Christian told him that if he cared for people and was kind to them, Christ would be there and come to him.

Offero decided to stay by a very deep stream in the mountains and help people across the stream. He did this because the stream was dangerous and people had been swept away and some had died. He was strong and with the help of a large stick and a light he got many people across the stream safely.

He hoped Jesus Christ would come and ask for his help. One day as it was getting dark a child came and wanted to cross the stream. The winter snows had been melting and the stream was very deep. Offero took the child's hand and they stepped into the cold water. But the water got too deep and Offero had to lift the child up and carry him in his arms. After a short while the stream was so deep Offero had to lift the child on to his shoulders. Even then the strong man had to struggle to get to the other bank. Once on the other side of the stream, Offero put the child down and began to dry himself. When he was a little drier and warmer he looked around but the child had gone. Offero then knew he had met the Christ. The child he had helped across the stream was Jesus Christ and he had come to Offero. He thought of the words that he had heard from the Bible. They were words that Jesus had said: 'Whoever welcomes one such child in my name, welcomes me.'

Offero got his name from carrying people across the stream. Now he was called Christoffero or Christopher, which means 'Christ carrier', because he had met and carried Jesus Christ.

Activity

Play 'In the river'. Everyone stands in a circle. One person stands in the middle. When she calls out, 'In the river', all have to jump forward. When she shouts, 'On the bank', all jump backwards. This sounds easy but there is a catch. If the caller shouts, 'On the river' or 'In the bank', no one must move. Anyone who even wobbles must sit out. The last person left is the winner.

Prayer

Jesus, we thank you that you loved children
and took them in your arms.
Help us to be kind and loving to each other.
Amen.

Song

Jesus' hands were kind hands

Notes

Christopher carries the Christ child

(a picture for colouring)

How can you help others?

For parents and children to pray together

'God, thank you for all who help us and care for us. May we help others also.'

Proper 21

Sunday between 25 September and 1 October inclusive

Aim

To encourage the group to learn to do good for Jesus.

Readings

Esther 7:1-6, 9-10; 9:20-22 or Numbers 11:4-6, 10-16, 24-29
Psalm 124 or Psalm 19:7-14
James 5:13-20
Mark 9:38-50

Teaching

Who knows the difference between salt and sugar? They look the same but they are quite different. Both are used at home in cooking. What foods do we put sugar into? What do we put salt into?

Sugar is used for making things sweet. It is used in cakes and in puddings.

Salt is used to help things taste good. It is often sprinkled on food – like chips, potatoes, eggs, or put into the pan when we are cooking things. I have some salt here to show you. (Produce a glass of water with salt dissolved in it.) Who can tell me where the salt is? It is in the water. It is hidden because it has melted, dissolved, in the water. How can we tell if there is salt in the water?

Nearly all cooked meat has salt in it. Sometimes meat that is not cooked has salt in it. Does anyone know why there is salt in it? It is to keep it from going bad; it stops the food spoiling and becoming nasty. Salt is used to keep it good. Salt is used to protect the meat and sometimes it is used to protect people.

Can you tell me where Jesus was born? He was born in a stable at Bethlehem. Fancy, Jesus being born in a stable among the cows and the donkey! (Describe the straw and get them to see it would not be all that clean.) The mother of Jesus would want to make sure Jesus was protected against any dirt and make sure he was kept safe. She would get Joseph to wash him and wrap him in swaddling bands (explain). But before he wrapped Jesus up, Joseph did something else to protect him. He gently rubbed salt on the body of the baby Jesus to keep him good and well and to stop any bad things happening to him. Our mothers and fathers would not use salt; they would use something gentler to protect us. But salt was what Joseph used because there were not so many medicines then. Just think how the little baby Jesus was given salt to keep his body healthy.

Jesus said we have to be like salt and to help to protect the world from bad things. We have to make sure we do not do bad things and upset our mothers or fathers. We should help to keep our rooms and our homes clean – and not expect our mother to do it all. We should not say nasty things or be horrible to anyone. This is not easy but we are to try and do it every day.

Let us see how many more ways we can be like salt and help to make our world a happier place. (Draw out suggestions from the children.)

Activity

'Sprinkled with salt.' Get the children to pretend to be angry or wanting to fight. Let them mime boxing and shaking fists. Then go around them pretending to shake salt on them. As they have salt on them, they are to go around shaking hands and hugging each other. Repeat this two or three times.

Prayer

Jesus, you want us to help you
by being good and caring for your world.
We will try to be helpful in our homes
and to be kind to others.
Amen.

Song

You are the best

Notes

Gives taste
Keeps things from going bad
Salt
Help people to enjoy life. Be good, kind, caring
Help to keep the world clean (or our room)
For parents and children to pray together.
'Lord God, thank you for the world and its nice things. May we try to keep it nice and beautiful. Amen.'

Proper 22

Sunday between 2 and 8 October inclusive

Aim
To show that God wants us to share in the care of his creation and to love one another.

Readings
Job 1:1; 2:1-10 or Genesis 2:18-24
Psalm 26 or Psalm 8
Hebrews 1:1-4; 2:5-12
Mark 10:2-16

Teaching
God made the world out of his love. When he made the human being he did not want him to be lonely, so God filled the world with wonderful creatures so that the man could look after them. God made all the animals on the earth, all the fish in the sea and all the birds of the air. God then brought them to the man so that he could give all the things a name and so that he could look after them. The man enjoyed giving names to cattle and to animals and birds. Let us see if we can name some of the animals God has made. (Look at the activity suggestion below.)

There were lots of wonderful things in the world but the man was still lonely; he needed a partner to share in looking after the world. He needed someone to love. So God made a partner for the man. Now the man not only had to care for the world, he also had to learn to love. He was not lonely any more. God made it so that we should all have people who love us and whom we love. Tell me who loves you and whom you love.

God wants us to look after his world and all that is in it. He wants us to show care for all the birds, the fish and the animals because he also cares for them. He wants us to care for the earth and the sea. He wants us to love him because he loves us.

How can we show we care for God's world? (Get ideas from the children. These could include tidying up and not throwing litter, being kind to animals, feeding the birds.)

And how do we show we love our mothers and fathers? (See if they can express a care for their homes, helping to tidy as well as doing what they are told.)

Activity
Have pictures of animals for the children to recognise. Include pets. See if they can name them. Then let the children choose a picture without telling anyone and make the sound of the creature. The rest of the group have to guess what it is. When it is guessed we all say, 'Thank God for . . .' and name the creature. On the activity sheet draw your favourite animal.

Prayer
Thank you, God, for a wonderful world,
for all the animals, birds and fish.
Thank your for our mothers and fathers
and thank you for making me.
Amen.

Song
God who made the earth

Notes

Say what these are and make the sound they make or show what they do.

For parents and children to pray together

'God, thank you for all the animals, for birds and fish. Help us to look after them always'

Draw your favourite animal

Proper 23

Sunday between 9 and 15 October inclusive

Aim

To show that Jesus wants all of us, not just our money or our prayers.

Readings

Job 23:1-9, 16-17 or Amos 5:6-7, 10-15
Psalm 22:1-15 or Psalm 90:12-17
Hebrews 4:12-16
Mark 10:17-31

Teaching

Once there was a little boy who lived with a very rich mother and father. He could have anything he wanted. He just had to ask and it was bought for him. He had all the toys he wanted and lots of nice clothes. When it came to his birthday he looked forward to having a party. Friends were invited and they had servants to look after them. Most of the children enjoyed themselves but the little boy was very sad. He had lots of friends and lots of presents but he felt lonely because his mother and father had gone away without him. What he wanted most was his mother and father, but they were always too busy and paid someone else to look after him. He wanted something more than presents; he wanted his parents to show they loved him . . .

Once a man came running to Jesus. The man was very rich and would have bought Jesus anything that he asked for. The man threw himself down at the feet of Jesus and asked how he might be given eternal life. The man would have bought eternal life, but Jesus knew you cannot buy it because it is a free gift from God. God does not want our money or gifts. Like the little boy in the story, God wants us to give ourselves to him; he wants us more than our gifts. When we give ourselves to God, God gives himself to us and gives us eternal life. When we come to church God wants us to give ourselves more than our collection, even more than our prayers – God wants all of us.

Activity

Let us look at the song 'Jesus wants all of me'. Say the words of the first verse and get the children to repeat them after you before you sing them.

Go through the second verse, getting them to point at each part of the body. Let them wave their hands, jump with their feet, swing their arms, shake their legs, wiggle their toes and knock their knees together. Go through the actions a few times before they attempt it to music.

End with shouting, 'What does Jesus want?' and let them reply loudly, 'Jesus wants all of me.'

Prayer

God, you give yourself to us.
We come to give ourselves to you.
As you love us, help us to love you.
Amen.

Song

Jesus wants all of me

Notes

The rich man turns away from Jesus

Write

Jesus
wants
all of
me

For parents and children to pray together

'Jesus, thank you for your love. We come to give our love and our life to you.'

Proper 24

Sunday between 16 and 22 October inclusive

Aim

To compare a king's life and the life of Jesus. (Use this as revision of what they know of Jesus.)

Readings

Job 38:1-7 (34-41) or Isaiah 53:4-12
Psalm 104:1-9, 24, 35c or Psalm 91:9-16
Hebrews 5:1-10
Mark 10:35-45

Teaching

Who knows what a king is? A king is a ruler of people and in Bible times he usually made them do what he wanted.

Where does a king live? He is usually born in a palace or a castle and that is where he lives.

Jesus is our King and he was born in a king's town. Where? Bethlehem. But he was not born in a castle. Where was he born? He was born in a stable among the cows and the donkeys. His mother's name was Mary. What do you call the day when Jesus was born? (Encourage all the children to say, 'Christmas Day'.) Jesus did not live in a palace; he lived in an ordinary house and worked in a carpenter's shop. (Make sure they know what a carpenter is.) Jesus would help to work with wood.

When Jesus grew up and left home he did not have lots of money or a rich house. He often slept outside in the countryside. He did not spend his time ordering people about, but he helped people and made ill people well again. All his life he cared for people.

A king sits on a throne and commands people, but Jesus was put on a cross (show a crucifix).

Who knows the name of the day when Jesus died? It is called Good Friday. (Encourage all the children to say, 'Good Friday'.) Jesus was given a crown but it did not have jewels in it and it was not made of gold. Who knows what it was made of? Encourage the children to talk about how painful it would be. Jesus came to give his life and his love for all people. He came as a king but a different king because he came to serve and to look after people. He wanted people to know that God loved them. A king would have called his army to fight but Jesus did not want to hurt or force people, so he died on the cross.

Jesus died, but after three days what happened? Yes, he was alive again. He rose from the dead. Does anyone know what we call the day when Jesus rose again? It is called Easter Day. (Get all the children to say, 'Easter Day'.) Because Jesus is alive he wants us to work with him and help him. He wants us to look after others. Let us think of things we can do for Jesus.

Spend the rest of the lesson making a list of suggestions of things that the children think they can do. Ask them to try and do at least one of them today.

Activity

Play 'The king says' version of 'Simon says'. Whoever is made king (or queen) commands people. When he says, 'The king says do this', he then does an action that the children must do. If the king gives an order without saying, 'The King says', no one should do what he does. Anyone who does is out and is relegated to the dungeons. The last one out becomes the next leader.

Prayer

Jesus, we thank you that you came to give your life for us.
Help us to give our life to you
and to care for others.
Amen.

Song

Jesus' hands were kind hands

Notes

Parents: use this sheet to ensure your child knows the names of the days in the life of Jesus.

Bethlehem

Born in a stable

Christmas day

Nazareth

Carpenter

Jesus

and disciples

Good Friday

Jesus is alive

Easter

For parents and children to pray together

'Jesus, you are our King, yet you gave your life for us. We come to give our love to you.'

Proper 25

Sunday between 23 and 29 October inclusive

Aim

To show Jesus giving sight to Bartimaeus.

Readings

Job 42:1-6, 10-17 or Jeremiah 31:7-9
Psalm 34:1-8, 19-22 or Psalm126
Hebrews 7:23-28
Mark 10:46-52

Teaching

Jericho was a very busy city. People were coming and going through its gates on the way to Jerusalem. There was a poor blind man called Bartimaeus. Can you say his name? That's right, Bartimaeus. Let us say it together once more.

Poor Bartimaeus, he was blind. His eyes could not see. He was always in the dark. (Touch your eyes and close them and shake your head.) He could not go around without bumping into things. Sometimes he held on to walls to know where he was going. Sometimes friends led him by the hand to take him to where he wanted to be. Most days his friends took him to the gate through which the main road went. There he sat with a bowl, begging. When he heard people passing by he cried out, 'Please help me! For the love of God, give me something!' (Act this out for the children to see.)

Because he was blind, Bartimaeus used his ears to listen more carefully. He listened to the noise of feet and to voices. He listened to friends who talked about Jesus and what he had been doing. He heard that Jesus made people well again and was speaking about God. Bartimaeus wondered if Jesus was the special One God had sent to bring peace and love to the world. Could Jesus be the Son of David who would put all wrong things right?

One day when he was sitting by the roadside he heard a great crowd coming and there seemed to be a lot of talking. Bartimaeus asked, 'Who is passing by?' They told him, 'Jesus is passing by.' Bartimaeus did not want to miss Jesus. He began to wave his arms and shout, 'Jesus, Son of David, please help me.' The people around him tried to make him be quiet. He waved his arms and shouted out again and again, 'Son of David, help me.' Let us wave our hands and shout like Bartimaeus, 'Son of David help me.'

Jesus heard Bartimaeus and stopped walking. He said, 'Let him come to me.' The people told Bartimaeus, 'Jesus is calling you.' He jumped up from his seat. He threw off his cloak in case it got in his way and with the help of the people he hurried to Jesus. Suddenly all was quiet and Bartimaeus heard Jesus saying in a very kind voice, 'What would you like me to do?'

What do you think Bartimaeus wanted most of all? Yes, he wanted to be able to see, so he said, 'Lord, make me see.' Then he hear the voice again, saying, 'Your faith has made you well.' Bartimaeus' eyes opened. He blinked in the sunlight. He could see Jesus in front of him. Bartimaeus could see. He could see people, he could see houses, he could see the road. He could see everything. He knew that Jesus must really be God's special One and he followed Jesus on the way.

Wasn't that wonderful? Jesus made the blind man see. Bartimaeus was lucky to meet Jesus and to know Jesus was God's Chosen One. Jesus is so kind and so clever he even makes the blind to see.

Activity

Have everyone stand in a circle. One person is blindfolded and placed in the middle. Turn them round a few times. They have to call 'Jesus'. A second person in the circle pretends to be Jesus and replies 'Timothy'. The blind person needs to keep calling until they find Jesus. Jesus must reply to each call.

Now let two more do the same.

Act out the story. Have a child for Jesus, a good few for the crowd (some can put money into the hands of Bartimaeus and others can tell him to be quiet), a child for Bartimaeus, two to help him to his place, and a child to say Jesus is passing by.

Prayer

For eyes to see, we thank you, God.
For colours and patterns, we thank you, God.
For the beautiful world and all its animals,
we thank you, God.
For books to read and pretty pictures,
we thank you, God.
For kind faces and good people, we thank you, God.
Amen.

Song

Two little eyes

Notes

On stiff paper or card, copy the face. Cut out the rectangles where the eyes and mouth should be. Cut slits in the sides.

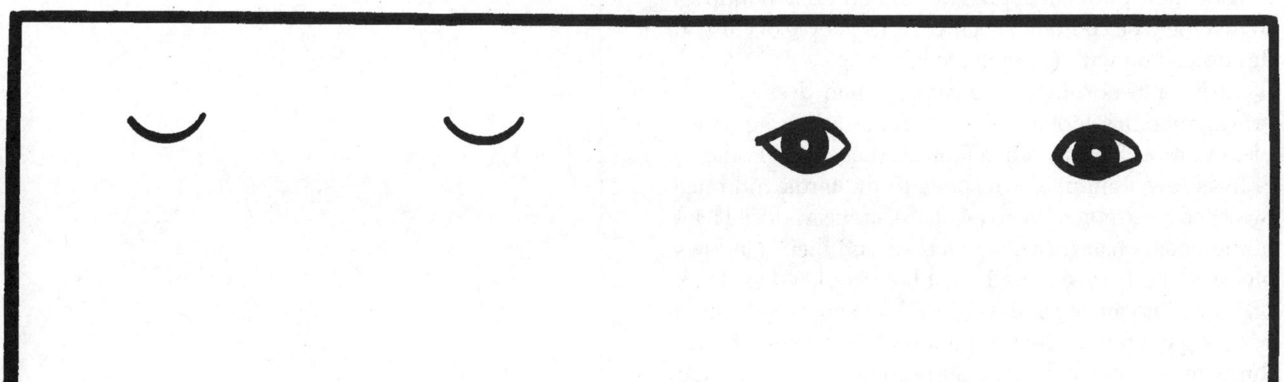

On a blank strip, draw in the eyes and mouth as shown.
Help the blind man to see

For parents and children to pray together

'Thank you, Jesus, for helping Bartimaeus.
Help us to see that you love us.

All Saints' Day

1 November
or Sunday between 30 October and 5 November inclusive

Aim

To tell the story of St Francis and the Wolf.

Readings

Wisdom 3:1-9 or Isaiah 25:6-9
Psalm 24:1-6
Revelation 21:1-6a
John 11:32-44

Teaching

At the beginning of the session play 'What time is it, Mr Wolf?' Encourage the wolf to growl as it chases the children. Then settle the children down.

Once upon a time in Italy there was a big bad wolf. Most of the time it lived in the forest near a place called Gubbio. (Let us all say 'Gubbio'.) The people who lived in Gubbio could not leave their hens or ducks or lambs out at night because of the wolf. If they did not shut their animals up, the wolf would come and steal them and eat them up. He was a big fierce wolf and he frightened the children and a lot of the grown-ups. If they saw him, they shouted at him and threw stones or sticks at him. They showed that they did not like him. They shouted loudly at him, and in turn he growled back at them. They were afraid to go into the wood at night in case they met the wolf. Some nights they could hear him howling but they were just as afraid when it was quiet because they did not know where he was. Before it got dark they used to shut their doors and put shutters on their windows so that the wolf could not get them. The people of Gubbio did not get on with the wolf at all.

Early one morning there came a man dressed in a brown robe. He looked very poor. For a belt he had a piece of rope. He was called Francis. (Let us say Francis.) Francis loved animals. He spoke to the birds and once preached a sermon to them (explain). Francis noticed a lot of the houses had their doors locked and their windows blocked out. He wondered what the people were afraid of. He had no money and he begged for some food. Often people gave him crusts or the food they were going to throw away. Whilst he was eating some bread, he asked what the people were frightened of. They told him about the wolf of Gubbio. They told him how it growled and how they threw sticks and stones at it. They often shouted at it to scare it away. Francis said he would go into the forest and try to find it and make friends with it. The people said it was very dangerous but Francis set off.

He had to look for a long time in the forest. He went right into where it was dark. Suddenly Francis heard a big growl. (Let us make a big growl. No, it was bigger and fiercer than that. Let us do it again.) The wolf thought it would frighten Francis but he spoke to it in a quiet voice and offered it a little of the food he was given. At first the wolf would not come. So Francis put some food down for it and moved away. The wolf could not understand because no one had ever been kind to it. Francis spoke to it gently with a friendly voice. He did not shout at it. He got it to eat some food from his hands. He stroked it and made friends with it.

As it was beginning to get dark, the people of Gubbio thought that perhaps the wolf had eaten Francis. Suddenly someone saw him coming out of the forest and following him like a dog was the big bad wolf. At first people were frightened but Francis persuaded them to care for the wolf, to feed it and not to shout at it. Because they did this the wolf of Gubbio became friendly and did not steal chickens, ducks or lambs. Everyone thought that Francis was brave and wise; that he was a man of God. They said Francis was a saint.

Activity

On the worksheet there is a stained-glass window with Francis and the wolf for colouring.

Prayer

God, we are happy that Francis was kind
to the birds and the wolf.
Help us to be kind to the birds and to all animals.
May we not do anything to hurt them.
Amen.

Song

Come on and shine

Notes

Saint Francis and the Wolf
For parents and children to pray together
'God, help us to be kind to the birds and the animals as St Francis was to the wolf.'

Fourth Sunday before Advent

Sunday between 30 October and 5 November inclusive
For use if the Feast of All Saints was celebrated on 1 November and alternative propers are needed

Aim

To encourage the children to show their love to God and to their parents.

Readings

Deuteronomy 6:1-9
Psalm 119:1-8
Hebrews 9:11-14
Mark 12:28-34

Teaching

Once upon a time there were two pretty kittens and they were given to a brother and sister. The girl's kitten was forever saying 'thank you' and showing its love. If she fed it, it sang to her. What is the sound it would make? It would purr. Let us all make the sound together. (Purr.) If she stroked it, again it would purr. (Get the children to make the sound.) If she cuddled it, it would make a lovely sound. (Purr.)

The other kitten did not think it was necessary to purr. The boy ought to feed me. He ought to stroke me. He should be giving me a cuddle. The boy did all these things but the kitten did not purr. It did not make a sound. After a long time of caring for the silent kitten, he started to cuddle his sister's kitten. Immediately it purred. He stroked it and it purred. He liked being with his sister's kitten because it showed you when it was happy and it sang 'thank you' when it was fed. He knew this kitten loved them but he was not sure of his own little kitten. He wanted to love it but he did not know if it loved him. It was lucky that the kitten soon realised what was wrong. It had failed to say 'thank you' or to appreciate that it was loved and cared for. It listened to the other kitten and it learnt to sing. It sang when it got its supper, it sang when it was cuddled, it sang when it was stroked. You could hear a wonderful sound all through the house, a sound that made the boy very happy. Let us make that sound.

Now, it is good to remember that our mothers and fathers look after us and love us. We must learn to say 'thank you' to them. To say 'thank you' for our meals and for their love and care. We do not want to be like the selfish kitten. We should tell our parents we love them and say 'thank you' for what they do for us.

God gave us a wonderful world to live in. He loves our parents and us. He wants us to show we love him. How can we do that? We could purr! But God made kittens to purr; he wants us to show we love him by coming to him in our prayers and by caring for his world and other people. Let us say together, 'Thank you, God, for loving us.'

We are not to live like the selfish kitten, so let us make a reminder to take home. It says on one side, 'Love God', and on the other, 'Love each other'. Let us say, 'Love God' together. Again. Now let us say, 'Love each other.' Again. Good, now let us say them one after the other: 'Love God. Love each other.'

Activity

There is a tag to make. The words are in outline. Let the children colour the words and then decorate the heart with glitter or with sticky stars (obtainable from most stationers).

Play musical statues. The children are to run around knowing God loves them. When the music stops they are to stand absolutely still; anyone who moves is pointed at and says, 'God loves me'. If they can say it, they stay in. (The youngest members may need to be encouraged to say it.) This is not an elimination game but one to help them to know and verbally express the love of God.

Prayer

God our Father,
we thank you for loving us.
We give you our love with all our heart.
Amen.

Song

Father, we adore you

Notes

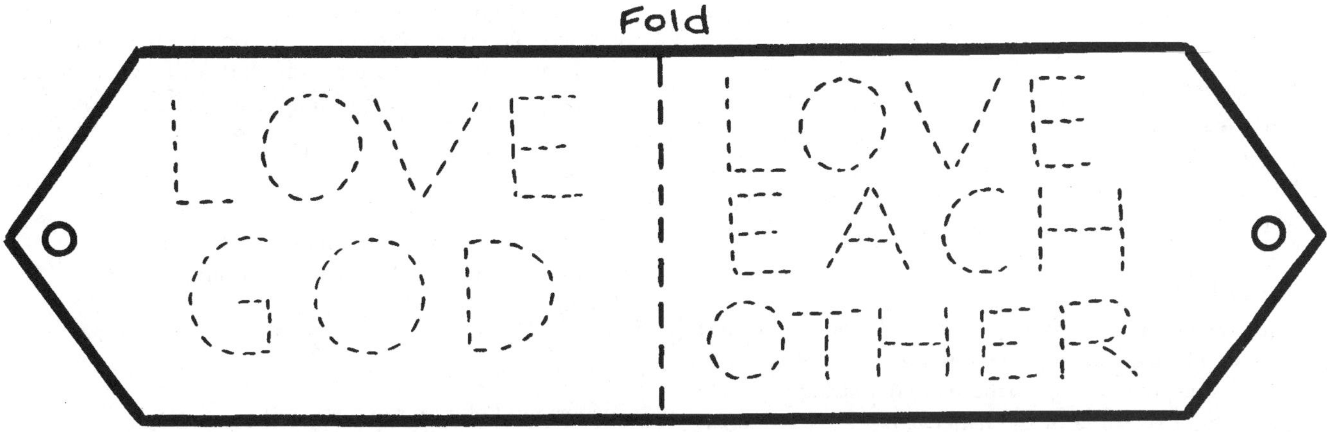

Join up the dots using different colours for each line. Decorate it all with glitter or sticky stars.
Then cut it out and fold it. Once folded, put a piece of wool through a punched hole.

For parents and children to pray together.

'God, we thank you for your love and for all the people who love us. Amen.'

Encourage your child to say:

Third Sunday before Advent

Aim

To know that Jesus called the disciples and he calls us too.

Readings

Jonah 3:1-5, 10
Psalm 62:5-12
Hebrews 9:24-28
Mark 1:14-20

Teaching

Jesus wanted people to help him to tell about God and his love. He needed people who would not give up, even when it was hard; people who were not afraid to work. He thought of some of the fishermen who worked on the Sea of Galilee. They were used to trying to catch fish, they did not give up, they worked hard and they were often very patient. They were not scholars or book men, they were not priests or holy men, but they were ordinary working men. Jesus thought it would be good if they would follow him.

Jesus went down to the seaside. It was in the morning and the fishermen were still busy. Andrew and Simon were still trying to catch fish. (Let us say their names: Andrew and Simon.) They had a net and they were throwing it into the sea and pulling it in. They were hoping to catch more fish, for they did not easily give up. They looked up and saw Jesus. He knew them and said to them, 'Follow me, and I will make you fish for people.'

Immediately, without asking any questions, they left their nets and followed Jesus. Now Jesus had two helpers. What were they called? (Andrew and Simon.)

A little further down the beach there was a group of fishermen with a large boat. There was a man called Zebedee. (Let us say it together: Zebedee.) He had two sons working with him and at this moment they were mending the nets. They had a special needle and some rope and were repairing the large hole in their net. There was also some men who worked with Zebedee. Jesus called to the ones he knew, James and John. (Let us say these names: James and John.) 'James and John, come and follow me.' Immediately they left their father Zebedee and the workmen and followed Jesus. Now he had four followers Andrew and Simon, James and John. (Let us say their names together: Andrew and Simon, James and John.) They were the first followers of Jesus.

Jesus still needs people to help him. He needs young people and old people. He wants them to bring others to him and show them how he loves them. He needs people who know him to follow him and tell others about him. We know the names of four disciples. Can we add our name to the followers of Jesus?

Activity

Cut fish out of card and put a paper clip on each fish. Cut a few people out of card and put a paper clip on their head. Divide the group into teams and give them a fishing rod that has a magnet on the end or a hook made from a paper clip. The idea is to transfer a fish from one end of the room to another and then to bring back a card person. (Each team will need at least two fish and two card people – and a monitor who continuously transfers the fish and people to the right end of the room.) The winning team is declared 'Champion Fishers of People'.

Prayer

Lord Jesus, I want to follow you.
I want to be a fisher of people.
I want to tell others that you love us all.
Amen.

Song

Fisherman Peter on the sea,
drop your net, boy, and follow me.

You may like to add the following verses:

> Andrew, his brother plain to see,
> leave your net, lad, and follow me.
>
> James and John, sons of Zebedee,
> stop your mending and follow me.

Notes

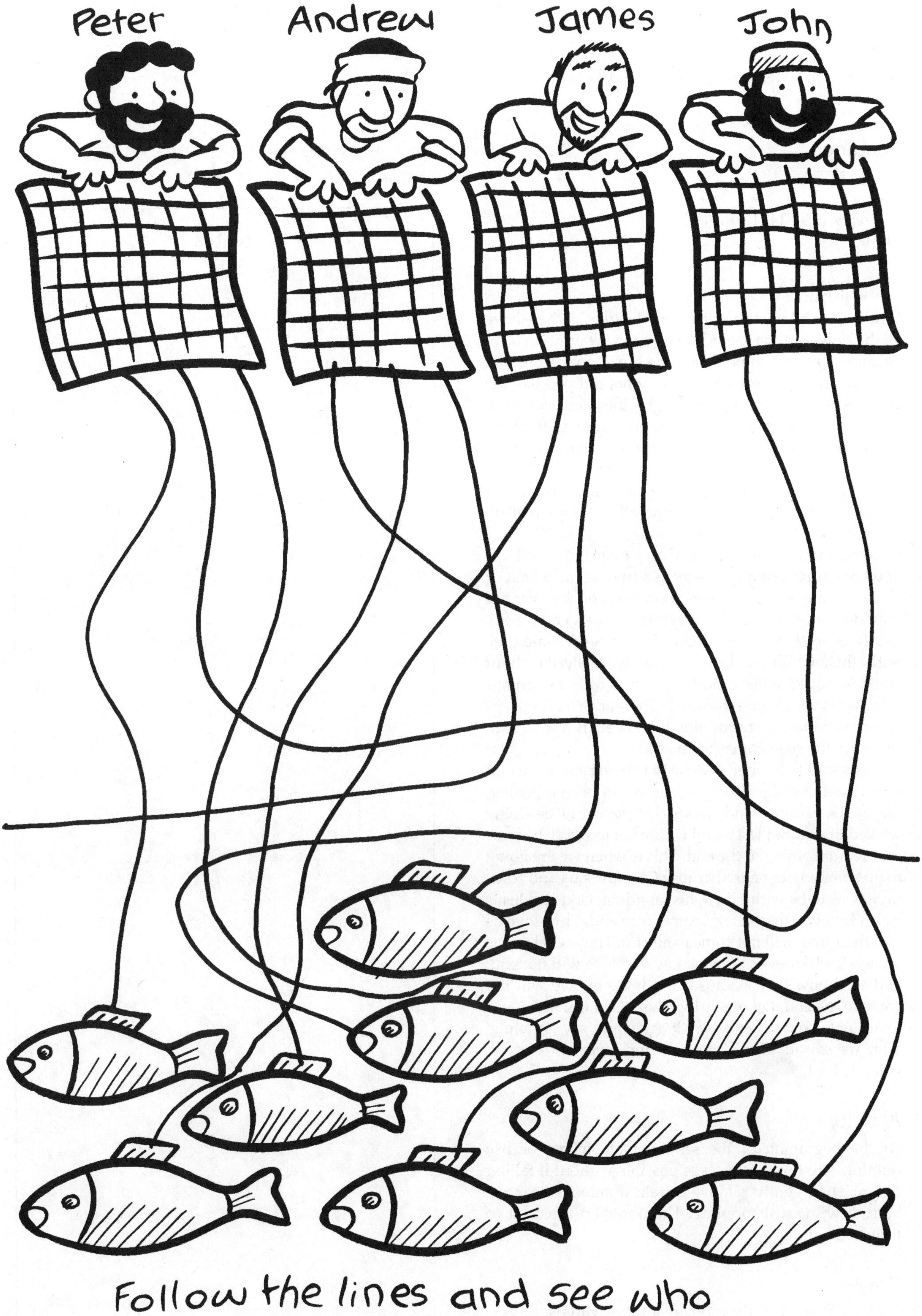

Follow the lines and see who will catch the most fish

Second Sunday before Advent

Aim

To show that whatever happens God is with us and loves us.

Readings

Daniel 12:1-3
Psalm 16
Hebrews 10:11-14 (15-18) 19-25
Mark 13:1-8

Teaching

Where have all the leaves gone off the trees? Where have all the flowers gone? Some have blown away, some have become fruit and some have been burnt on the bonfire. If you went to a firework display, what did you like the best? Some fireworks went right into the sky with sparkles and sounds. What were they called? Rockets. Then some made big bangs and threw flames in the air before they went out. None of them lasted for hours. Some things do not last long at all, like pocket money or chocolates. Can you tell me some other things that do not last?

Some things seem to last a very long time. Perhaps you have travelled a long way in a train, a car, a boat or an aeroplane. Some journeys seem to go on for ever but they do come to an end. Everything has an end – well, nearly everything. (You might like to spend some time with this. Children are not usually bothered about endings, not even life's end.) Sometimes we get warnings that things are coming to an end. The smoke alarm peeps when its batteries are running low. There is a road sign that says the road comes to an end.

Jesus said that when the world was coming to an end we would see signs. Bad things could be happening, like wars, famines and floods. People could be doing wicked things. But Jesus said we are not to worry because we are not coming to the end. This is when we are going to go somewhere better because God loves us and Jesus invites us to be with him in his kingdom. God and Jesus go on for ever; they do not come to an end. They love us and their love will not come to an end. They will love us always and for ever. So we know that love will not end, and we know that, because God loves us, we will not come to the end. Let us say together; 'God is with us and loves us for ever.' Let us say it again and say, 'Alleluia' after we say it. 'God is with us and loves us for ever. Alleluia.'

Activity

At the beginning of the session play 'Jenga' or use dominoes to build as high as possible without it falling down. Then gently remove certain dominoes near the bottom without it toppling. The one who causes it to topple is out.

Prayer

God, we thank you that you are always with us,
that you love us and care for us.
We give our love to you.
Amen.

Song

Jesus' love is very wonderful

Notes

Colour the words. Say them together. Decorate the heart with glitter and stars.
Cut it out and hang it up at home.

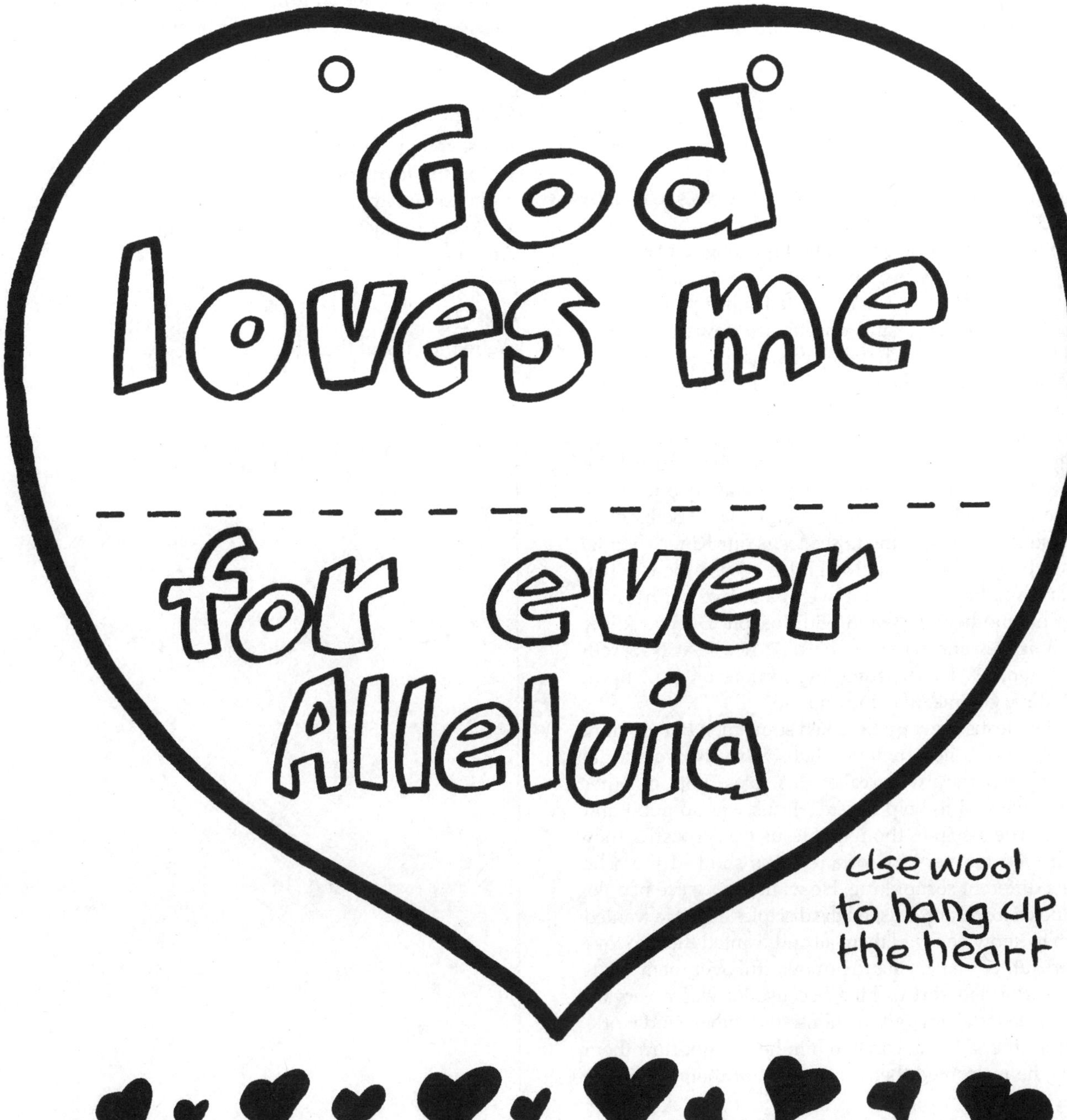

For parents and children to pray together

'God, thank you for your love. You care for us and always look after us. We give our love to you. Amen.'

Christ the King

Aim

To enjoy the reality of Christ as our King. To use this as a time of checking on what the children know of Jesus.

Readings

Daniel 7:9-10, 13-14
Psalm 93
Revelation 1:4b-8
John 18:33-37

Teaching

Who knows who is our queen? Where does she usually live? Kings and queens live in palaces and have lots of servants. What else do you know about kings and queens? They have crowns, usually made of gold and jewels. They are usually very rich and tell other people what they must do. Kings and queens are powerful people and make others do what they command.

We have a King who is very different from most kings. He is more powerful but he does not make us do things. He wants us to do things because we love him. Our King was not born in a palace, not even in a house. Who can tell us our King's name? Where was he born? In a stable. And what was the name of the place? Bethlehem. Do you know who came to see Jesus our King when he was a baby? The shepherds and the wise men. When Jesus was a boy, he did not live in a palace but he lived with his mother Mary and with Joseph. Do you know where it was and what Joseph did? It was at Nazareth and Joseph was a carpenter (explain). Jesus grew up in an ordinary home, like you and me.

When Jesus grew up he asked some men to help him. Do you know how many? There were twelve special helpers and they were called disciples. Lots of other people wanted to help because Jesus was so good and loving. The disciples thought if Jesus was powerful they might become very important. Jesus showed them he was a different sort of king. He wanted to serve people. He took a towel and washed the disciples' feet. He wanted them to know he loved them all and wanted them to love others rather than trying to be powerful over them. Jesus was a different sort of king because he was a Servant King. He was always giving himself for others and working for others. If any came to him he did not turn them away; he welcomed them and cared for them. He is the King of love.

Our King had to fight against evil but he did not want to use force; he wanted to win by showing his love. The evil people put him to death. Who knows how Jesus died? He died on a cross and he had a crown on his head but it was not a crown of gold; it was a crown of thorns (explain). After Jesus died he was buried in a cave, but on the third day what happened? Jesus rose again. He was alive and his disciples saw him. Jesus the King had won the battle against evil and death and is alive for ever.

Jesus is our King. He loves us and wants us to be his friend. Jesus wants us to speak to him each day. He wants us to be children of the King and to love him as he loves us.

Activity

Make crowns out of gold paper and add jewels to them. Play 'Pass the crown'. Let it go from head to head. When the music stops, whoever is wearing the crown must say, 'We are children of the King.' Everyone else says, 'Alleluia' and waves their hands. The music starts again and the game continues.

Prayer

Jesus, you are our King.
Help us to love you
and to do what you want us to do.
We know that you love us and care for us.
Amen.

Song

We're the kids of the King

Notes

Colour the jewels and add them to the crown.
It would be good to use gold paper for the crown and add sticky stars and glitter.

How many crowns can you find?

For parents and children to pray together

'Jesus, you are our King and you love us. Help us to love you and to do what you want us to do.'

xxx ♥ xxx